AIR CAMPAIGN

MALTA 1940–42

The Axis' air battle for Mediterranean supremacy

RYAN K. NOPPEN | ILLUSTRATED BY GRAHAM TURNER

OSPREY

Bloomsbury Publishing Plc
PO Box 883, Oxford, OX1 9PL, UK
1385 Broadway, 5th Floor, New York, NY 10018, USA
E-mail: info@ospreypublishing.com
www.ospreypublishing.com

OSPREY is a trademark of Osprey Publishing Ltd

First published in Great Britain in 2018

© Osprey Publishing Ltd, 2018

A catalogue record for this book is available from the British Library.

ISBN: PB 9781472820600; eBook 9781472820624; ePDF 9781472820617; XML 9781472826046

18 19 20 21 22   10 9 8 7 6 5 4 3 2 1

Maps by bounford.com
3D BEVs by The Black Spot
Diagrams by Adam Tooby
Index by Alan Rutter
Typeset by PDQ Digital Media Solutions, Bungay, UK
Printed in China through World Print Ltd

Artist's note

Readers may care to note that the original paintings from which the colour plates in this book were prepared are available for private sale. All reproduction copyright whatsoever is retained by the publishers. All enquiries should be addressed to: Graham Turner, PO Box 568, Aylesbury, Bucks, HP17 8EX, UK, or www.studio88.co.uk

The publishers regret that they can enter into no correspondence upon this matter.

Front Cover: Art by Graham Turner © Osprey Publishing
Back Cover: Photo courtesy IWM

Osprey Publishing supports the Woodland Trust, the UK's leading woodland conservation charity. Between 2014 and 2018 our donations are being spent on their Centenary Woods project in the UK.

To find out more about our authors and books visit www.ospreypublishing.com. Here you will find extracts, author interviews, details of forthcoming events and the option to sign up for our newsletter.

Reference guide

Regia Aeronautica Organization:
Sezione – four fighters, or three bomber or other types of aircraft, depending on the type of unit; basic Regia Aeronautica tactical combat unit
Squadriglia – three Sezione
Gruppo – three Squadriglie of fighters, two Squadriglie of bombers or other aircraft
Stormo – two Gruppi
Brigata Aerea – two Stormi
Divisione Aerea – three Stormi
Squadra Aerea – two or three Divisione Aerea or Brigata Aerea covering a specific territory

Regia Aeronautica Abbreviations and Terms:
C.T. – *Caccia Terrestre*, or land based fighters
B.T. – *Bombardamento Terrestre*, or land based bombers
B.a.T. – *Bombardamento a Tuffo*, or dive bombers
R.S.T. – *Ricongnizione Strategica Terrestre*, or land based strategic reconnaissance
A.S. or Sil. – *Aerosiluranti*, or torpedo aircraft

Luftwaffe Organization:
Rotte – two fighters (leader and wingman); basic Luftwaffe fighter tactical combat unit
Kette – three bombers; basic Luftwaffe bomber tactical combat unit
Schwarm – two Rotten of fighters
Staffel – three Schwärme or Ketten
Gruppe – three Staffeln
Geschwader – three to four Gruppen
Fliegerkorps – several Geschwadern; basic Luftwaffe operational combat unit
Luftflotte – one or more Fliegerkorps

Luftwaffe Abbreviations and Terms:
JG – *Jagdgeschwader*, or fighter wing
ZG - *Zerstörergeschwader*, or heavy fighter wing
KG – *Kampfgeschwader*, or bomber wing
StG – *Sturzkampfgeschwader*, or dive bomber wing
LG – *Lehrgeschwader*, or experimental/instructional wing
TG – *Transportgeschwader*, or transport wing
Aufkl.Gr. – *Aufklärungsgruppe*, or reconnaissance group

Author's note

The focus of this text is upon the Regia Aeronautica's and Luftwaffe's air campaign to impose a state of aerial denial upon the Royal Air Force on the island of Malta through the neutralization of its aircraft and aerial infrastructure. Regia Aeronautica and Luftwaffe interdiction efforts against British Mediterranean shipping and convoys are treated as a separate air campaign and are not examined in this text

CONTENTS

INTRODUCTION

Aerial view of Valletta and Malta's Grand Harbour from 1938. Note the large concentration of Royal Navy capital ships and the floating dock, all tempting targets to Mussolini who hoped to displace British influence in the Mediterranean. (NARA)

In the late 19th century, the Mediterranean became the naval linchpin of the British Empire, connecting India and the Far East to the British Isles. At the centre of the Mediterranean lay the island of Malta, home of the Royal Navy's largest squadron outside British home waters, the Mediterranean Fleet. By the early 20th century, Malta's Royal Navy Dockyard possessed the most extensive docking and repair facilities outside the British Isles. At the time, Britain's expanding naval facilities in the Far East did not have graving docks capable of accommodating the Royal Navy's larger capital ships, leaving Malta as the closest fully-equipped naval base. As Malta was ten days' sailing time from Britain, warships were ten days closer to the Far East, making Malta an ideal base for forward deployment.

The Royal Navy had paid little attention to the defence of Malta, let alone the Mediterranean, in the years between the wars. After all Britain remained allied to the two largest Mediterranean naval powers, France and Italy. Throughout the late 1920s and 1930s however, Italy's *Duce*, Benito Mussolini, who had become Prime Minister in 1922, became increasingly discontent with the territorial status quo in the Mediterranean and sought to expand the boundaries of his fascist state.

Beginning in 1926, Mussolini confided to his military leaders that it was his desire to have free access to the oceans. He had decided to breathe new life into the concept of *Mare Nostrum*, championed in the previous generation by imperialists Francesco Crispi and Gabriele D'Annunzio. At first Mussolini looked to expand Italian territory in the Balkans and Africa but he came to realize, and increasingly told his generals and admirals so, that Italian hegemony in the Mediterranean could only be achieved by eventual conflict with France and Britain. A window of opportunity to act upon these designs came nine years later in 1935, when Adolf Hitler publically announced his programme of German rearmament. As the attention of France and Great Britain was drawn towards the unexpected threat of a militarily resurgent Germany, Mussolini believed the time had come to test the resolve of the great powers. Italian leaders had long had designs on Abyssinia, adjacent to the Italian colony of Somaliland. Using a border incident between Abyssinian troops and Italian askaris

IDROVOLANTI S.55 X-SAVOIA MARCHETTI ➤ MOTORI ASSO DA 750 HP.
ISOTTA FRASCHINI ➤ MAGNETI, CANDELE E BATTERIE DELLA MAGNETI MARELLI ➤
CARBURANTE PER AVIAZIONE STANAVO DELLA SOC.ITALO-AMERKANA PEL PETROLIO-GENOVA

Poster for the *Crociera Aerea del Decennale 1933*, a mass flight of 25 SM.55 flying boats from Italy to New York to Chicago and back. The Regia Aeronautica used mass flights throughout the 1930s to inflate the perception of air power and prestige of Mussolini's regime. (collection of the author)

in December 1934 as a pretext, Mussolini began a large military build-up in Eritrea and Somaliland in the spring of the following year. While the League of Nations attempted to arbitrate the dispute between the two nations throughout spring and summer, Mussolini secretly instructed his military commanders to prepare for war.

His military commanders were stunned at the seemingly cavalier attitude Mussolini took regarding a potential war with Britain, as Italy was in no position to take on the world's strongest naval power alone. Immediately recognizing the threat posed by British forces based on Malta, Admiral Domenico Cavagnari, Chief of Staff of the Regia Marina, initiated a feasibility study of an amphibious invasion of Malta, but planning never developed beyond generic preliminary studies. In reality, a combined-arms operation involving coordinated naval/air operations and amphibious landings was then beyond the capabilities of the Italian armed services. Since his first years in power Mussolini had discouraged effective coordination between the armed services due to his fear of coordinated military opposition to his rule. The *Stato Maggiore Generale*, or Supreme General Staff (known colloquially as

Mussolini walking in front of a line of new SM.81 bombers during the Abyssinian Crisis. Aware from British intelligence intercepts that the Royal Navy perceived the aircraft as a threat to the Mediterranean Fleet, Mussolini had the few SM.81s then in service make a number of highly publicized flights. (ullstein bild via Getty Images)

Comando Supremo) governed the strategic directives of the armed services in name, but in practice the separate branches operated independently, answering only to Mussolini. Inter-service rivalries further developed due to their intense competition for defence spending. Cavagnari advised Mussolini that a combined-arms operation against Malta would serve little purpose since the British were likely to base their fleet at Alexandria or Gibraltar, well beyond the operational radius of the Regia Marina and Regia Aeronautica. Instead he reasoned that the only way to offset superior British naval strength in the Mediterranean was an immediate heavy strike on the British Mediterranean Fleet and naval and air facilities at Malta with Regia Aeronautica bombers, followed by bombing British vessels as they withdrew from Malta to either end of the Mediterranean. As far as Cavagnari was concerned: let the Regia Aeronautica take the responsibility and the risk.

General Giuseppe Valle, *Capo di stato maggiore dell'Aeronautica* or Chief of Staff of the Regia Aeronautica, likewise recommended a heavy aerial attack against targets on Malta and in the Central Mediterranean. Eager to prove the capabilities of an independent air arm, Valle initially boasted that his aircraft would drop 100 tons a day on the island. But this was largely bravado to impress Mussolini; Valle was skeptical about the success of a sustained aerial campaign against Malta due to the limited loads that his bombers could carry, as well as their obsolescent performance. A new generation of bombers was being designed, but the Regia Aeronautica would have to go to war with antiquated types such as the Caproni Ca.101 transport/bomber and the Savoia-Marchetti S.55 flying boat. Over the course of the summer of 1935 both Cavagnari's and Valle's staffs continued to draw up separate plans for attacks on Malta but both were forced to acknowledge that the navy and air force did not have the ability to carry out sustained operations beyond the Central Mediterranean. Following high-altitude bombing exercises against naval targets conducted by the Regia Aeronautica during the summer, Valle tried to convince Mussolini not to go to war; bombing accuracy was too poor and its light bombs judged to be ineffective against enemy warships. Nevertheless on 3 October 1935, Mussolini unleashed his invasion of Abyssinia.

In spite of all its bellicose rhetoric and frantic military planning, the British took no military action against Italy and the invasion of Abyssinia proceeded unhindered. In internal discussions, the British government concluded that an Italian conquest of Abyssinia had little or no impact on the affairs of the Empire, but a rhetorical gesture had to be made in order to prop up the League of Nations. More pressingly, Britain discovered during the summer of 1935 that its Royal Navy and Royal Air Force were ill-prepared for a war against a determined Italian adversary. The Mediterranean Fleet, the largest force of British ships outside home waters, was sitting at anchor at Malta only 60 miles from Italian air bases in Sicily, a flying time of only 30 minutes. RAF reconnaissance flights recorded the arrival of several Regia Aeronautica bomber units in Sicily throughout the summer. At the time Malta had only six anti-aircraft guns on the entire island, and no RAF squadron was permanently based on its airfield. Fearful of a surprise attack, the British Admiralty decided to move the Mediterranean Fleet to Alexandria, out of range of Italian aircraft, a process which began at the end of August. The British gradually improved their overall military position in the Mediterranean during the course of the war in Abyssinia but Whitehall had long come to the conclusion that it was more politically expedient, militarily prudent, and cost-effective to avoid any unnecessary conflict with Italy.

Back in Rome, Mussolini was much less anxious throughout the Abyssinian crisis than the British leadership. His seemingly reckless course of action was in fact based on detailed knowledge of British intentions and military capabilities. The *Servizio Informazioni Militari* (Military Intelligence Service), or SIM, had cracked several British ciphers and its operatives had gained access to the British embassy in Rome. From wide-ranging information disseminated from intelligence reports, Mussolini concluded that the British were unwilling to go to war with Italy over Abyssinia, particularly as the British government still hoped to depend on Italy as an additional counterweight to German militarism. Of particular interest was the revelation that the Royal Navy was closely following the development of the Regia Aeronautica's new monoplane bomber, the Savoia-Marchetti SM.81, an aircraft that had a 200-mile operational radius with a 2,000kg bombload. Intercepted British reports repeatedly stated British concerns that the SM.81 could render Malta's naval facilities useless through heavy aerial bombardment. Although the SM.81 was just entering series production when the Italians invaded Abyssinia, the Regia Aeronautica held a number of aerial displays with the handful in service and heavily publicized the aircraft, hoping to further exacerbate British fears. Because of the SIM's intelligence coup, Mussolini knew exactly how far he could push the British without any serious retaliation.

This diplomatic victory was tempered by the realization that an eventual war with Britain and France would require military assets that Italy simply did not possess in 1935–36. In order to one day fully assert Italian authority in the Mediterranean, Mussolini dramatically increased military spending for all services and embarked on a rearmament programme in the middle of the Abyssinian Crisis. Wrestling control of the Mediterranean from Britain and France would require a powerful navy and air force, both of which would have to operate beyond the central Mediterranean. Given the limitations of the Italian economy and armaments industry, Italy's military leadership calculated that it would likely take at least seven years to prepare such forces. In the meantime Mussolini contented himself by militarily supporting the fascist forces of General Francisco Franco in the Spanish Civil War from 1936 to 1939, intent on creating an ally at the western end of the Mediterranean, right next to the British stronghold of Gibraltar. Furthermore in April 1939, Mussolini annexed the Kingdom of Albania, giving Italian forces a foothold in the Balkans for future operations against Yugoslavia and Greece. By the summer of 1939 Mussolini may have been achieving aggressive foreign policy successes in preparation for his planned Mediterranean hegemony, but the Regia Aeronautica was still a long way from being ready for further aggressive moves in the Mediterranean. Between 1935 and 1940, the Regia Aeronautica faced a number of problems that stunted rather than enhanced its development and operational effectiveness, and which would greatly plague its performance as it embarked upon a campaign to neutralize Malta's aerial and naval infrastructure in the summer of 1940.

CHRONOLOGY

1940

April–May Six crated Gloster Sea Gladiators are assembled at Hal Far airfield, forming Malta's only fighter unit.

29 May Italy's first dive-bomber unit formed with the Savoia-Marchetti SM.85 and prototype SM.86

10 June Italy declares war on Britain and France.

11 June 55 SM.79s and 18 C.200 fighter escorts carry out the first bombing raids on Malta, followed by 38 SM.79s that afternoon. It would be the heaviest day of bombing for months, with 43,000kg of bombs dropped.

12–25 June Small bombing raids flown against Malta, one of which cripples the Royal Navy's giant floating dock in Valetta.

21–22 June Five Hurricanes arrive at Hal Far.

25 June Armistice between France and Italy comes into effect.

15 July Serious problems having been found with the SM.85 dive bomber, 96° Gruppo B.a.T. pilots are sent to the Luftwaffe's Stukaschule 2 in Graz to train on the Ju 87 Stuka.

4–5 August CR.42s fly fighter sweeps against Malta; RAF fighters scramble but climb to the south to avoid unnecessary combat.

5 September The Regia Aeronautica launches its first precision dive-bombing strikes against the island with Ju 87s.

9 September The Italian campaign in Egypt begins; some of the SM.79 bomber units on Sicily are withdrawn and sent to North Africa to assist.

27 September Dive bombers of 96° Gruppo B.a.T. are withdrawn to Lecce on mainland Italy

28 October Italy invades Greece and more bomber units are withdrawn from Sicily to assist; 12 RAF Wellingtons of No. 148 Squadron are ordered to Malta to begin trial bombing in Italy and North Africa.

10 November A reconnaissance flight from Malta confirms Italian battleships are in Taranto harbour; in the subsequent raid Swordfish from HMS *Illustrious* disable three of them.

20 December Mussolini forced to appeal to Hitler for assistance in the Balkans and Libya.

1941

10 January The Luftwaffe makes its debut in the Mediterranean when X Fliegerkorps conducts its first attacks, targeting the Royal Navy's Force A; the Stukas damage aircraft carrier HMS *Illustrious*, which is forced into Valetta for emergency repairs

11 January Hitler outlines his priorities for X Fliegerkorps in Weisung Nr. 22, including keeping the Strait of Sicily closed to British shipping, preventing the Royal Navy from disrupting Axis convoys to North Africa, attacking British naval and port facilities in Egypt and Cyrenaica, and supporting ground operations in North Africa.

16–19 January Raids target *Illustrious* in Valetta docks and the fighter airfields; *Illustrious* suffers only minor damage and leaves on 23 January.

3 February Admiral Raeder recommends an invasion of Malta at a meeting with Hitler.

12 February Bf 109s escort X Fliegerkorps' bombers for the first time, shooting down two Hurricanes.

26 February Sixty bombers escorted by single- and twin-engined fighters attack Luqa, causing heavy damage to airfield and aircraft.

27 March Coup d'état against pro-Axis government in Yugoslavia leads to Hitler ordering an invasion; German priorities switch away from Malta to the Balkans.

Late April Last large-scale raids hit Malta before most of X Fliegerkorps' bombers leave for Greece in May.

27 April–20 May Bf 109s of III/JG 27 are temporarily posted to Sicily; with 7/JG 26 they shoot down 14 Hurricanes and strafe in addition to routine escort duties.

12 May Hurricane-equipped No. 185 Squadron formed at Hal Far.

1 June Air Commodore Hugh Pughe Lloyd appointed commander of AHQ Malta; initiates massive ground defence-building programme for airfields.

June Hurricane-equipped No. 249 Squadron and No. 46 Squadron (renamed No. 126 Squadron on 30 June) arrive by carrier.

Mid-June Luftwaffe units are all transferred to other theatres; the Regia Aeronautica is the only air force on Sicily.

1 October Italy's Macchi C.202 fighter makes its combat debut over Malta.

December II Fliegerkorps arrive in Sicily.

19–31 December Escorted Ju 88s carry out the first Luftwaffe attacks of the new campaign and are soon averaging around four daylight raids per day. Thirteen Hurricanes are destroyed in combat and another 16 RAF aircraft on the ground by the end of 1941.

1942
4 January RAF Blenheims and Wellingtons raid Castelvetrano, destroying 12 aircraft and damaging 42.

January–March Priority is given to eliminating RAF bombers on Malta, raids are flown as weather permits.

Early March RAF on Malta reduced to 21 operational Hurricanes; Axis now has air superiority over Malta and the central Mediterranean.

7 March First 15 Spitfires arrive on Malta; a further nine arrive on 21 March.

20–21 March A series of major raids puts Takali airfield out of action.

22–23 March The airfields are given a brief reprieve while Luftflotte 2 focuses on sinking Convoy MW10.

1 April Despite reinforcements of ten Hurricanes from North Africa on 27 March and another nine Spitfires on 29 March the RAF is reduced to a handful of operational fighters.

2–30 April An average of two Luftwaffe heavy raids are flown per day against Malta, typically of 30–70 bombers with escort.

19 April Seven more Hurricanes arrive from North Africa.

21 April 46 more Spitfires arrive, flown off HMS *Eagle* and USS *Wasp*.

21 April Hitler agrees to an Italian-led, German-supported invasion of Malta and orders German planning to begin under the codename Operation *Herkules*.

9 May With the RAF nearly crippled by airfield bombing, 60 more Spitfires arrive off HMS *Eagle* and USS *Wasp*.

10 May Kesselring declares air superiority over Malta; Luftflotte 2 begins to be redeployed.

Mid-June The Luftwaffe presence on Sicily is reduced to 27 Bf 109Fs, 21 Ju 88s, and the reconnaissance aircraft of 1/Aufkl.Gr. 121.

15 June Reconsidering his support for an invasion of Malta, Hitler refuses an Italian request for the fuel required.

21 June Hitler suspends Operation *Herkules*.

November With Rommel's defeat at El Alamein and the Allies' *Torch* landings, the Luftwaffe and Regia Aeronautica send most of their remaining forces in Sicily to North Africa.

ATTACKERS' CAPABILITIES 1940
The Regia Aeronautica

Doctrines and leadership

Fiat CR.32 fighters in flight during the Spanish Civil War. The combat success of the CR.32 in the skies over Spain led to Italian misconceptions about the sustained viability of the biplane configuration with regards to new fighter development. (Ministero della Difesa)

A fundamental question has to be asked at this point: was the Regia Aeronautica capable of undertaking an independent aerial campaign in which decisive results could be achieved by air power alone when Italy went to war in 1940? Could an objective such as neutralizing Malta or compelling the British garrison to surrender be achieved through aerial attack and bombardment alone?

While Valle was forced to reluctantly admit his doubts during the Abyssinian Crisis, he believed that this was due to a lack of necessary aircraft – not that Italian air power was incapable of achieving decisive results within a campaign, or even strategic results within a conflict. Throughout the 1930s the Regia Aeronautica's leadership remained wedded to the strategic bombing theories of General Giulio Douhet: that a large air force alone, with command of the air and equipped with a large number of bombers, could win campaigns by the destruction of an enemy's will to fight through the area bombing of population and industrial centres, i.e. terror bombing. This was despite the fact that the Regia Aeronautica had not equipped its bomber squadrons with large bombers since the large Caproni Ca.3 series of World War I. Only a handful of prototypes were experimented with during the interwar years but none entered production.

The ultimate reason for Italy's lack of heavy bombers was that the Regia Aeronautica simply could not afford to build and maintain a large force of such aircraft, even with the increased spending under Mussolini. With a national income only around 50 per cent of France's and around 25 per cent of Britain's, the Italian economy was in no shape to subsidize a force of expensive heavy bombers; even the substantially more robust French and British economies struggled to afford them during the late 1930s. Valle insisted upon maintaining the operational independence of the Regia Aeronautica, claiming that Douhetian strategy could be undertaken by acquiring numerous smaller, more affordable tactical bombers. This would allow Valle to build up a numerically strong air force while remaining free from the influence of the army or navy. The inter-service rivalries heavily influenced Valle's decision-making process.

Cost and rivalry were not the only factors in Valle's decision to pursue a medium bomber-building programme however. He and other Regia Aeronautica officials were compelled to take notice of the alternative theories being espoused by fellow officer General Amedeo Mecozzi. In stark contrast to Douhet, Mecozzi believed that strategic bombing alone could not determine the outcome of a conflict and that given Italy's limited economic means, possession of a large fighter force to take strategic command of the air alongside a strong heavy bomber arm could not be a financial reality. Instead he believed that the role of the air force was to achieve local air superiority over a target and support the army and/or navy in tactical operations through assault tactics. This would require a balanced force made up of fighters, assault (i.e. 'attack') aircraft, and medium bombers. Assault and bomber pilots would be trained in *volo rasente* ('skimming flights' – low-level attack tactics and horizontal bomb release at 50m altitude) and glide bombing (low-angle diving bomb release) tactics, both of which delivered accurate strikes at low altitude on individual targets such as troop concentrations, defensive positions, vehicles, airfields, depots, warships, etc. Given the lack of large urban and industrial targets within its projected Mediterranean theatre of operations, Mecozzi further emphasized Italy's need for a tactically oriented air force. To neutralize Malta's offensive potential, Regia Aeronautica bombers would have to target airfields, anti-aircraft guns, bunkers, warehouses, dry-docks, warships, etc. – accurately and regularly. Mecozzi's tactical ground attack theories found favour with enough officers within the Regia Aeronautica to compel Valle to order the design and production of purpose-built assault aircraft for the Regia Aeronautica, beginning in 1934.

Valle approved of both the financial aspect of Mecozzi's emphasis on medium bombers and his realistic appraisal of potential enemy targets in the Mediterranean. However, Mecozzi's firm belief in inter-service cooperation and combined-arms operations, and most importantly subordination of control of air assets to ground and sea commanders during combat operations, completely fell on deaf ears. Valle fiercely defended the independence of the Regia Aeronautica and, despite growing evidence to the contrary, defended his force's ability to independently undertake large strategic operations. Valle claimed that accurate strikes made by assault aircraft were simply a method by which to more efficiently achieve air supremacy over a target prior to heavy bombardment. To the Regia Aeronautica chiefs Mecozzi's theories did not discredit Douhet's; rather, they were simply redefined as a component of greater Douhetian strategic theory. Thus the selective simultaneous application of Douhet's and Mecozzi's theories left the Regia Aeronautica without a sound or uniform operational doctrine, except for an ingrained desire to undertake campaigns on its own.

The insistence upon Douhetian theory with a relatively small force of medium bombers, coupled with a half-hearted appreciation for Mecozzi's assault theories, left the Regia Aeronautica in a strategic vacuum with regard to combat operations. Italian combat experience in the Spanish Civil War actually led to erroneous conclusions about how to respond to the changing nature of modern aerial warfare. One of these conclusions was restricting medium bombers to horizontal attacks at higher altitudes. Bomber pilots experimented with bombing attacks at low altitude in conjunction with Mecozzi's ground strike theories, achieving greater accuracy but increasing the risk of damage to their aircraft from anti-aircraft fire. Regia Aeronautica tacticians calculated that horizontal attacks made in formation at high altitude would likely result in adequate damage to a target at much lower risk to the attacking aircraft – and, from a cost point of view, decrease the risk of losing an expensive weapons platform. Payloads had to be limited to around 1,000kg however, as additional weight dramatically affected the climb and stability of medium bombers. In practice, this resulted in an inaccurate dispersal of a relatively light bomb load.

General Giulio Douhet, the air power theorist whose doctrines held sway over many pre-war Regia Aeronautica commanders and strategists. (collection of the author)

General Amedeo Mecozzi, who offered a counterpoint to Douhet's theories, arguing for the development of a tactically-minded air force made up of fighters, assault aircraft, and medium bombers. (collection of the author)

Capo di stato maggiore dell'Aeronautica General Giuseppe Valle (front, right), Chief of Staff of the Regia Aeronautica from 1933–39, speaking with General der Flieger Erhard Milch of the Luftwaffe at the II° Salone Internazionale Aeronautico Milano in October 1937. (Archivio Storico Fondazione Fiera Milano)

A second erroneous conclusion was the continued adherence to high-manoeuvrability dogfight tactics after the seeming vindication of the biplane in the skies over Spain, where Italian pilots achieved a higher kill ratio than their foes. This gave the biplane fighter unrealistic consideration in future wartime planning. Biplane-era high-manoeuvrability tactics continued to be taught and encouraged, even though new low-wing monoplanes could not be handled in combat in the same manner. A number of training accidents caused by aerobatic manoeuvres unsuited to monoplanes as well as a lack of proper training left many Regia Aeronautica fighter pilots with a reluctance to convert to monoplanes in 1939, in spite of overwhelming foreign acceptance of the type. Another false conclusion was the tangible effectiveness of area/terror bombing. Italian bombers undertook several area/terror bombing missions over Madrid and Barcelona, with the purpose of destroying military targets and damaging both military and civilian morale, which the Regia Aeronautica viewed as public demonstrations of Douhetian air power. The Regia Aeronautica leadership refused to acknowledge that the bombardments had no lasting effect on the campaigns against those cities or on the civilian populations within, and instead basked in the lavish praise Mussolini extended to the air force for demonstrating Italian military might to the world.

Valle's successor and the commander of the Regia Aeronautica when Italy entered World War II, General Francesco Pricolo, spoke about a pressing need for inter-service cooperation on the eve of the conflict, but like his predecessors he remained committed to a Douhetian view of air power. Pricolo had been an advocate of the terror bombing raids against cities during the Spanish Civil War, believing that such raids would break the morale of urban defenders. When they did not, Pricolo responded that it was not due to a failure in the theory but rather a lack of political will, in the face of foreign criticism, to conduct a terror bombing campaign for long enough to achieve the desired results. Pricolo considered a similar campaign against Malta to force the island's surrender, but in early June 1940 the Comando Supremo instructed him to avoid attacks on civilian targets; aware that Italy's anti-aircraft defences were minimal at best, Comando Supremo did not want to provoke a British and French aerial bombardment of Italian cities, even for a short war. Thus ironically Mussolini's government, out of fear of being on the receiving end of Douhetian terror bombing, refused to allow the Regia Aeronautica to employ the tactics it had so long espoused and by which it believed air power alone could decide campaigns. Despite this operational limitation, Pricolo believed that aerial bombardment of Malta's military, naval and aviation facilities and the continued threat thereof (hence relying on terror) would deter the British from basing offensive units there, effectively neutralizing the island's offensive potential and imposing a state of aerial denial.

Capo di stato maggiore dell'Aeronautica General Francesco Pricolo (to the right of Mussolini), the Regia Aeronautica's first wartime commander, inspecting a unit of SM.79s with Mussolini before Italy's entry into the war. (Public domain via Wikimedia Commons)

Aircraft

To accommodate Mussolini's military ambitions, in August 1936 the Regia Aeronautica undertook a comprehensive study with the aim of creating an escalated production programme that would expand the number of combat aircraft based in Italy and the Mediterranean basin to 3,000 (five times the number that were in service in late 1934) over a relatively brief period. It was intended that at least two-thirds of the new 3,000-strong air force would be made up of new types and to that end the Regia Aeronautica organized several new aircraft design competitions. In an attempt to fully evaluate all of the new designs the Regia Aeronautica delayed implementation of its *Programma R* (R Programme) acquisition plan until December 1939, but the start of World War II forced it to move production forwards. From 1936 to 1939 the Regia Aeronautica nevertheless placed a number of orders for new aircraft while its planners mulled over the composition of the R Programme. Some of the newer designs used transitional construction methods while the Italian aviation industry prepared for all-metal construction and enhanced the performance of its domestically engineered engines.

Unfortunately for the Regia Aeronautica, Mussolini brought Italy into the war during this time of transition when the air force had not yet completed its expansion through the R Programme (unrealistically scheduled to be completed in the second half of 1940), and neither had the aviation industry completed preparations for a new generation of fighters, bombers, and engines. The failure of the Italian aero industry to design and build new, high-quality radial engines, and the Regia Aeronautica's failure to encourage further development of up-to-date inline designs, would dramatically limit the performance and operational capabilities of its pre-war generation of aircraft.

Fiat BR.20

Before planning for the R Programme even began, General Valle realized that his bomber arm was in desperate need of a new generation of modern, purpose-designed bombers and ordered the *Direzione Generale delle Construzioni e degli Approvvigionamenti* (General Directorate of Construction and Procurement, or DGCA) of the Regia Aeronautica to set forth new specifications, which in his mind successfully melded both Douhet's and Mecozzi's

BR.20 bomber prototype on display at the II° Salone Internazionale Aeronautico Milano in October 1937. (Archivio Storico Fondazione Fiera Milano)

operational theories. The specification requirements of the subsequent 1934 modern bomber competition were for a twin-engine aircraft with a maximum speed of 240mph at 16,500ft, carrying a payload of 1,000kg, a defensive armament of three machine guns, and retractable landing gear. The only design to fully meet this criteria was the Fiat BR.20 *Cicogna* (Stork), which was ordered into production in 1936. Although the BR.20 was clearly the superior aircraft among the competition's entrants, the Regia Aeronautica also placed orders for two other competition entries – the Caproni Ca.135 and the Piaggio P.32 – even though their performance fell short of the air force's requirements. The Regia Aeronautica ordered these to have 'back-ups' in case of developmental problems.

All of the aircraft were underpowered, primarily due to their unreliable 1,000hp Fiat A.80 and 1,000hp Piaggio P.XI radial engines; both had lower power-to-weight ratios than their foreign equivalents and required more frequent maintenance. The overall performance of the Caproni Ca.135 and Piaggio P.32 proved to be so poor that both aircraft were taken out of Regia Aeronautica service by 1939. The BR.20's superior flight characteristics kept the aircraft in service and new cooling, exhaust, and lubrication systems for the troublesome A.80 engines were incorporated into the later BR.20M model which went into production in 1940. By the end of 1940, however, most of the initial production models of the BR.20 were already out of service, relegated to secondary roles.

BOMBERS OF THE REGIA AERONAUTICA			
	Fiat BR.20M Cicogna (stork)	CANT Z.1007 *bis* Alcione (kingfisher)	Savoia-Marchetti SM.79 Sparviero (sparrowhawk)
Length	53ft ¾in (16.2m)	61ft ¼in (18.6m)	53ft 2in (16.2m)
Wingspan	70ft 8¾in (21.6m)	81ft 4½in (24.8m)	66ft 3in (20.2m)
Powerplant	2× 1,000hp Fiat A.80 R.C.41 radial engines	3× 1,000hp Piaggio P.XI bis R.C.40 radial engines	3× 780hp Alfa 126 R.C.34 radial engines
Maximum speed	270mph (430km/h)	285mph (458km/h)	270mph (430km/h)
Range	1,196 miles (1,925km)	1,243 miles (2,000km)	1,130 miles (1,820km)
Ceiling	24,934ft (7,600m)	27,559ft (8,400m)	21,325ft (6,500m)
Armament	3× 12.7mm Breda-SAFAT machine guns	2× 7.7mm and 2× 12.7mm Breda-SAFAT machine guns	1× 7.7mm and 3× 12.7mm Breda-SAFAT machine guns
Payload	3,530lb (1,600kg)	4,850lb (2,200kg)	2,756lb (1,250kg)
Crew	5	5	5

Savoia-Marchetti SM.79

The two bombers that would see extensive service over Malta were not selected from a Regia Aeronautica design competition but were designs converted from civilian transport aircraft. The first, the Savoia-Marchetti SM.79 *Sparviero*, was a trimotor originally designed as a high-speed, long-range passenger aircraft for the MacRobertson Air Race of 1934. Ironically the Regia Aeronautica initially did not see the military potential of the aircraft, its attentions being fixed on the twin-engine prototypes of the 1934 bomber competition. It was only after Savoia-Marchetti made a convincing case following a series of informal talks with the air force leadership that an order for 24 aircraft was placed in early 1936. The SM.79 was powered by three 780hp Alfa Romeo 126 R.C.34 radial engines. Although offering less horsepower than the Fiat A.80 and Piaggio P.XI radials, the Alfa 126, itself developed from licence-produced Bristol Pegasus radials, was more reliable as it was not greatly altered from the original British design. As the SM.79 was tested against the BR.20 in 1935 and into 1936, the flight characteristics of the SM.79 proved to be superior. The SM.79's three engines gave it a greater power-to-weight ratio and better manoeuvrability. As the limitations of the BR.20's two Fiat A.80 engines became increasingly apparent after the aircraft entered service, the increased reliability afforded by the trimotor configuration of

the SM.79 became the aircraft's primary selling point; the SM.79 could fly on two engines if one failed or was damaged.

This surviving SM.79 is preserved in the Museo Storico Aeronautica Militare in Vigna di Valle. (Alan Wilson/ CC BY-SA 2.0)

Although the SM.79 had a lower maximum payload than the BR.20 (2,756lbs compared to 3,530lbs), its engines required less maintenance and allowed the SM.79 to operate longer between engine overhauls. By the spring of 1938 only 98 BR.20s had been produced compared to 179 SM.79s, demonstrating the Regia Aeronautica's preference for the trimotor. Furthermore by the end of the year the Regia Aeronautica had assigned SM.79 production to the Macchi and Reggiane firms. With a maximum speed of 270mph, the SM.79 was faster than most foreign medium bombers of the time but Savoia-Marchetti's use of mixed construction materials (wood, steel and fabric) made the aircraft somewhat dated, as foreign manufacturers were turning more and more to all-metal construction.

CANT Z.1007 *bis*

The second Regia Aeronautica bomber to see significant service over Malta was the *Cantieri Aeronautici e Navali Triestini* firm's CANT Z.1007 *bis Alcione*, a landplane design developed in 1935 from the three-engine CANT Z.506 transport floatplane. Eighteen Z.1007s were ordered by the Regia Aeronautica in early 1936, followed by another 16 in early 1937, even though the design was still on the drawing board; as with the SM.79, the Regia Aeronautica was eager to test new medium bomber designs following the disappointing results of the 1934 competition. The Z.1007 prototype, powered by three 830hp Isotta Fraschini Asso XI RC15 inline engines, first flew on 11 March 1937. Although the aircraft was underpowered, its streamlined wooden airframe gave it overall good performance and the trimotor configuration guaranteed greater operational reliability. The Regia Aeronautica was impressed enough to encourage further development of the project and CANT redesigned the aircraft, making it larger in order to accommodate three 1,000hp Piaggio P.XI R.C.40 radial engines. The first redesigned CANT Z.1007 *bis* took its first flight on 6 June 1939. The Z.1007 *bis* was a fast bombing platform, having a higher maximum speed (285mph) and ceiling (27,559ft) as well as a larger payload (4,850lbs) than the SM.79. It had one significant drawback however: it was constructed primarily out of wood, resulting in a complex and lengthy construction method as well as chronic maintenance problems. By June 1940 only 34 Asso-powered

The prototype of the
CANT Z.1007 with three
830hp Isotta Fraschini
Asso inline engines.(Public
domain via Wikimedia
Commons)

Z.1007s and 34 Z.1007 *bis* were in service. Even before the Z.1007 *bis* entered production both it and the SM.79 were seen as transitionary aircraft due to their wooden components and third engine, the weight of which restricted additional defensive armament, armour protection, and payload. As long as the reliability of Italian-produced engines remained in doubt the Regia Aeronautica felt compelled to rely on trimotor designs.

Savoia-Marchetti SM.85

The strike theories of Amedeo Mecozzi finally saw tangible consideration when the Regia Aeronautica began testing its first dive bomber, the Savoia-Marchetti SM.85. It was a twin-engine mid-wing monoplane of wood and fabric construction with an internal bomb bay and retractable landing gear. It was powered by two 460hp Piaggio P.VII C.35 radial engines, armed with a single 7.7mm or 12.7mm machine gun, and could carry a 500kg bomb. The prototype first flew in December 1936 and it was found that the aircraft was severely underpowered; it climbed very slowly, even after bomb release, and it could not fly with full fuel tanks when loaded with its 500kg bomb. Despite this poor performance the need to get a dive bomber into service compelled the Regia Aeronautica to order 48 examples in 1938. The first SM.85s came off the production lines in March 1939 and in subsequent testing were found to still have poor performance, tended to shake violently in a dive, and some even went into uncontrollable spins during a dive. Already in 1937 Savoia-Marchetti had designed an improved dive-bomber, the SM.86, the prototype of which first flew on 22 September 1937.

The SM.86 had a larger wing and new cockpit, and was powered by two 600hp Walter Sagitta IC-SR engines, giving the aircraft a higher maximum speed, increased rate of climb, and the ability to carry a 500kg bomb with a full fuel load. The SM.86 was put through a series of rigorous tests and the Regia Aeronautica was interested enough in the project to order additional prototypes. Production of the SM.85 was allowed to continue until

A line-up of new SM.85 dive bombers at a pre-war display. The poor performance of this aircraft allowed the advocates of Douhetian theory in the Regia Aeronautica to minimalize the pre-war development of dive bomber and assault aircraft. (NARA)

December 1939 so that new dive-bomber pilots would have an aircraft to train on while the Regia Aeronautica waited for the finished development of the SM.86 project. As far as the Regia Aeronautica's Douhetian leadership was concerned, the mediocre performance of the SM.85, coupled with negative pilot reports of two other ground-attack aircraft under development in the late 1930s – the Breda Ba.65 and Breda Ba.88 – cast shadows over the effectiveness of dive-bombing missions; the tangible evidence to the contrary achieved by German Junkers Ju 87s in Spain was conveniently ignored. The Regia Aeronautica ordered production of the SM.85 halted in May 1940 after 34 had been produced, but it allowed the existing aircraft to enter service as it had no alternative dive bomber. To this end the R Programme created only one Stormi of dive bombers compared to 26 Stormi of medium bombers.

Fiat CR.42

In November 1936 the Regia Aeronautica announced a new fighter contest and issued specifications for both a new biplane fighter and a new monoplane fighter in preparation for the R Programme. Regia Aeronautica planners were aware of foreign air forces' preference for developing monoplane fighters and what modern monoplanes in the hands of skilled pilots could do, having witnessed firsthand the success of early-model Messerschmitt Bf 109s in Spain. Nevertheless there was a determination to continue investment in biplane development due to the successes that Italian Fiat CR.32 biplane fighters had in tight turning dogfights against the much faster Soviet-built Polikarpov I-16 monoplane fighters – which were largely due to Soviet and Spanish Republican inexperience in the handling characteristics of monoplanes, and in high-speed hit-and-run monoplane combat tactics. Beyond the tactical preferences of its pilots and the success of the CR.32 in Spain, the Regia Aeronautica's justification was that it believed that a period of time would be required to adequately train pilots on a completely new type of aircraft that was just entering production; the biplane component of the 1936 fighter contest was designed to find an aircraft with superior performance to the CR.32, but one which pilots would find to be a familiar combat platform as they transitioned to new monoplanes (the monoplane component of the contest).

To this end, on 10 February 1938 the Regia Aeronautica ordered 200 examples of the Fiat CR.42 biplane fighter, a design that was still on the drawing board and the prototype of which did not fly until 23 May 1938 – in fact the prototype of its rival in the biplane competition, the Caproni Ca.165, first flew on 16 February 1938. Fiat used its political muscle, claiming the need to keep its assembly lines busy, to secure the Regia Aeronautica

This CR.42, part of the Corpo Aereo Italiano stationed in Belgium in 1940-41, made a forced landing in Suffolk on 11 November 1940 and has belonged to the RAF ever since. It is now on display at the Royal Air Force Museum in Hendon. (collection of the author)

OPPOSITE AXIS AIRFIELDS ON SICILY AND PANTELLERIA

contract. Fiat's lines in fact were busy, producing 337 of the increasingly obsolescent CR.32 for export sale or as replacements for those deployed to Spain between January 1938 and May 1939. While the CR.42 proved to have impressive performance for a biplane, it pushed the biplane configuration to its technological limits. Fiat showed little concern for this as long as it could compel the Regia Aeronautica to purchase the CR.42, and the aircraft had excellent export potential; this was the time of the general Continental rearmament drive following Germany's annexation of Austria in the autumn of 1938, and a number of smaller European air forces were eager to purchase any relatively modern aircraft.

FIGHTERS OF THE REGIA AERONAUTICA			
	Fiat CR.42 Falco (falcon)	Macchi C.200 Saetta (arrow)	Macchi C.202 Folgore (thunderbolt)*
Length	27ft 1in (8.3m)	27ft 1in (8.3m)	29ft ½in (9m)
Wingspan	31ft 10in (9.7m)	34ft 8in (10.6m)	34ft 8½in (10.5m)
Powerplant	840hp Fiat A.74 RC38 radial	840 hp Fiat A.74 RC38 radial	1× 1,085hp Alfa Romeo RA.1000 R.C.41-I Monsone inline
Maximum speed	272mph (438 km/h)	312mph (503km/h)	373mph (600km/h)
Range	481 miles (775km)	354 miles (570km)	478 miles (769km)
Ceiling	32,970ft (10,050m)	29,200ft (8,900m)	37,740ft (11,500m)
Armament	2× 12.7mm Breda-SAFAT machine guns	2× 12.7mm Breda-SAFAT machine guns	2× 7.7mm Breda-SAFAT machine guns
Crew	1	1	1
* Introduced October 1941			

Macchi C.200

The Regia Aeronautica selected Macchi's C.200, the best overall performer, as the winner of its monoplane fighter competition. The prototype first flew on 24 December 1937, and for a monoplane it was very manoeuvrable, a trait that would endear it to Italian pilots, and it had a maximum speed of 312mph, making it the fastest Italian fighter yet produced. When compared to contemporary British and German inline-engined monoplane fighters, however, the C.200 was either considerably slower or significantly under-armed, or both. The Supermarine Spitfire Mk I, powered by a 1,030hp Rolls Royce Merlin III engine, had a top speed of 367mph and was armed with eight .303in machine guns while the Hawker Hurricane Mk I, also powered by a Merlin III engine, had a top speed of only 318mph and was armed with eight .303in machine guns. The Messerschmitt Bf 109E, powered by a 1,085hp DB 601A-1 engine, had a top speed of 354mph and was armed with two 7.7mm machine guns and two 20mm cannon. The primary reason for the C.200's lesser speed and armament was its 840hp Fiat A.74 RC38 radial engine's lack of power, although at the time this Fiat engine was the most powerful, yet reliable, engine available in quantity to Italian airframe manufacturers. When Macchi began design work on its C.200 project in 1935, it was originally intended to arm the fighter with five machine guns and power it with the then-new 1,000hp Fiat A.80 radial engine. When the serviceability problems of the A.80 engine became apparent the following year, Macchi was forced to turn to the more reliable A.74, but the planned armament had to be cut for the aircraft to have reasonably competitive performance.

Macchi received an initial production order for 99 C.200s in the summer of 1938 and contracts for licence production were awarded to Breda and SAI Ambrosini the following

SARDINIA

Tyrrhenian Sea

ITALY

Taranto

Crotone

Ionian Sea

Reggio di Calabria

Palermo

Trapani

Chinisia

Casrelvetrano

Sciacca

SICILY

San Pietro a Caltagirone

Gerbini

Catania

Comiso

Gela

Strait of Sicily

Pantelleria

MALTA

TUNISIA

N

50 miles

50km

This surviving C.200 was captured by the British Army in Benghazi in November 1942 and shipped to the United States; it is preserved in the National Museum of the United States Air Force. (collection of the author)

year. Production of the all-metal airframe was to prove challenging for firms that had little of the specialized equipment or experience required for mass production, resulting in a 20,000-hour production time for a single Macchi C.200; for comparison, it took 4,500 hours to build a Bf 109E. While the C.200's airframe offered the possibility of further refinement of the fighter, the lack of a more powerful engine prohibited further development. Out of desperation for a more powerful engine, the Regia Aeronautica began negotiations with Daimler-Benz in the summer of 1939 to purchase a licence for Alfa-Romeo to produce the 1,085hp DB 601A-1 inline engine, a deal which was struck that November. A few DB 601A-1 engines were purchased directly from Daimler-Benz and distributed to several aero manufacturers, including Macchi, so that development could begin on a new generation of inline-engined fighters. As it took a full year for Alfa-Romeo to retool for manufacture of the new engine, production and use of the C.200 had to continue. The slow construction of the monoplane meant that the CR.42 would have to be used to round out the number of fighters required for the R Programme, leaving the Regia Aeronautica with two different types of fighters that demanded fundamentally different approaches to combat training.

Despite years of investment, development, and new production, a close inspection of the Regia Aeronautica at the time World War II began showed an air force that desperately needed re-equipping from its operations in the Spanish Civil War. Sixty-six per cent of the Italian military's budget from 1935 to 1940 was spent solely on military operations in Abyssinia, Spain, and Albania, with domestic rearmament having to be funded out of the remaining 34 per cent. On the surface however its commander painted a very different picture. Throughout the late 1930s General Valle, eager to please his leader and perhaps all too eager to cover up any perceived mismanagement, had grievously overestimated the potential of the Regia Aeronautica to Mussolini. Suspicious of reports to the contrary, Comando Supremo ordered a thorough inventory of the Regia Aeronautica's aircraft, equipment, and stores in September 1939, and began to find that Valle's appraisals were far from the truth. Mussolini was initially reluctant to believe that the air force was in such a poor state, unwilling to recognize that it was not the modern and efficient service that Valle had optimistically claimed for so long, but eventually dismissed the air force commander on 31 October 1939.

The true combat readiness of the Regia Aeronautica was finally uncovered when General Pricolo received the full inventory and analysis completed by the *Direzione Generale dei Servizi del Ministero dell'Aeronautica* on 1 November 1939. Valle had documented an air force of 8,530 aircraft of which 5,948 were considered combat aircraft including ten different types of fighters, 11 types of bombers, four types of observation aircraft, and 11 types of floatplanes and seaplanes – a logistical nightmare. Breaking down the total figure of combat aircraft, it was discovered that Valle had included 2,534 non-existent aircraft – the yet-to-be-built aircraft of the R Programme – bringing the total of tangible aircraft to 3,414. Out of the tangible total it was discovered that only 2,802 aircraft were in service, the remainder being in storage or consigned to flight schools, and only 1,691 of these were operational (although 179 aircraft in reserve at *Squadra Riparazioni Aeromobili e Motori*, or Aircraft and Motor Repair Unit, depots could quickly be made operational when crews were made available). Finally out of the total 2,802 combat aircraft in service, there were only

536 bombers (388 SM.79, 148 BR.20) and 191 fighters (143 CR.42, 19 G.50, 29 C.200) that could be considered modern, and of these only 396 bombers and 129 fighters were seviceable; hardly a number with which to enter a protracted war with Britain and France across a front as broad as the Mediterranean. As to the high percentage (40 per cent) of non-operational Regia Aeronautica aircraft in General Pricolo's November 1939 investigation, the primary reasons were a lack of trained mechanics, and that the production of aircraft and engine spare parts lagged significantly behind the production of new aircraft. Given the mess that was inherited from Valle, there was little Pricolo could do to improve the Regia Aeronautica's operational readiness and effectiveness, as well as its combat strength, in the immediate present.

By early June 1940 new construction brought the number of combat aircraft from 2,802 in November of the previous year to 3,619, including 323 aircraft based in Italian East Africa. Of the 3,296 aircraft based in Italy and the Mediterranean basin, 1,796 were considered operational (plus 520 aircraft in reserve at Squadra Riparazioni Aeromobili e Motori depots). With 46 per cent of its aircraft non-operational, the personnel and logistics situation of the Regia Aeronautica clearly had not been improved since November 1939. The total number of operational modern fighters and bombers including those in East Africa had however increased to 574 and 900 respectively, including:

Fighters	
Fiat CR.42	300 (202 operational, 12 in reserve, and 86 under maintenance and repair)
Macchi C.200	156 (77 operational, 43 in reserve, and 36 under maintenance and repair)
Fiat G.50	118 (89 operational, 12 in reserve, and 17 under maintenance and repair)
Bombers	
Savoia-Marchetti SM.79	594 (403 operational, 36 in reserve, and 155 under maintenance and repair)
Fiat BR.20	219 (132 operational, 31 in reserve, and 56 under maintenance and repair)
CANT Z. 1007 bis	87 (38 operational, 18 in reserve, and 31 under maintenance and repair)

This meant a total of 368 operational modern fighters and 573 modern operational bombers spread across the entire Italian Empire. The Regia Aeronautica had 130,950 tons of aviation fuel at storage depots, air bases, and at private commercial facilities that was distributed by tanker vessels, railway tank cars, or in barrels by truck. It was calculated that 130,950 tons could sustain six months of aerial operations.

In terms of explosive ordnance, the Regia Aeronautica's stocks included the following:

800kg	20
500kg	444
250kg	1,073
100kg (high explosive and semi-armor piercing)	5,817
50kg	6,738
small anti-personnel bombs (2kg–15kg)	46,686
incendiary bombs (2kg–20kg)	9,039

As with its fuel stores, the Regia Aeronautica only had enough explosive ordnance for several months of combat (calculating that the average operational payload for an Italian medium bomber was 1,000kg).

DEFENDERS' CAPABILITIES 1940
Britain's Central Mediterranean outpost

Strategic requirements

At the end of August 1935, amid the growing tensions of the Abyssinian Crisis, most of the British Mediterranean Fleet sailed from its base at Malta to the port of Alexandria in Egypt in order to remove its important units from the threat of surprise air attack from Sicily. The fleet remained at Alexandria for the duration of the crisis and returned to Malta in the middle of the following year. Despite the extensive development of the Royal Navy Dockyard and other naval infrastructure in Valetta's Grand Harbour over the years, in August 1936 the Royal Navy arranged to develop Alexandria as a wartime base for the Mediterranean Fleet in the event of war with Italy. There was some debate regarding the subsequent usefulness of Malta's naval facilities during future hostilities and some wondered whether a defence of the island should be attempted at all given the threat of Italian air attack.

However, in March 1937 the Committee of Imperial Defence, or CID, decided that Malta would remain the primary base of the Mediterranean Fleet in peacetime as it would take years to construct adequate facilities for wartime operations in Alexandria. In times of war Malta would support light forces such as cruisers, destroyers, and submarines due to the island's proximity to Italian sea lanes to North Africa. The Royal Navy felt comfortable basing light forces at Malta as a result of continued analysis of the Regia Aeronautica's actual anti-shipping capabilities. By the spring of 1936, the Royal Navy and Royal Air Force realized they had grossly overestimated the attack capabilities of the Savoia-Marchetti SM.81, particularly when it came to attacks on warships. Realizing that the Regia Aeronautica's bomber arm still adhered to a policy of attacking warships from a high altitude (roughly 15,000ft), British experts calculated that SM.81s had only a very small chance (less than 1 per cent) of any of their bombs hitting a defensively manoeuvring warship from high altitude. Intelligence reports of subsequent Italian anti-shipping exercises in the years leading up to the war showed that the Regia Aeronautica continued to use the same high-altitude tactics with its newer SM.79 and CANT Z.1007 *bis* bombers. The Royal Navy felt that the ability to raid Italian sea lanes with light units was worth the risk of exposing these vessels to what was seen as largely ineffective aerial bombardment. To this end the Royal Navy strongly pushed for the establishment of an effective aerial defence of Malta.

Air defences

The first aerial facility on Malta was the seaplane base at Kalafrana on the western shore of Marsaxlokk Bay, opened in July 1916 to support Royal Naval Air Service floatplanes and flying boats flying patrols against German and Austro-Hungarian U-boats. Throughout the interwar years it was used as a base by rotating RAF seaplane squadrons conducting anti-submarine patrols, anti-piracy patrols, reconnaissance flights, and air-sea-rescue operations. An airstrip was constructed at Hal Far on the southeastern end of the island in 1923 to provide a shore base for Fleet Air Arm (FAA) carrier aircraft. Originally thought of as an extension of Kalafrana, Hal Far was opened as a permanent RAF station on 31 March 1929. During the early 1930s Hal Far was used primarily by disembarked carrier flights from 802 Squadron (Nimrods), 812 Squadron (Ripons), and 823 Squadron (Fairey IIIFs and Seals).

Before World War II Hal Far had no permanent squadrons; given the limited number of aircraft that Hal Far could handle, the RAF was not keen on exposing a handful of squadrons to surprise attack by a Regia Aeronautica force that could number into the hundreds. As a token defence during the Abyssinian Crisis, No. 74 Squadron (12 Hawker Demon two-seater fighters) and No. 22 Squadron (12 Vickers Vildebeest torpedo bombers) were stationed at Hal Far, but these squadrons were sent back to England in the summer of 1936, the British government not being willing to antagonize the Italians once the crisis had passed. Further Italian sabre-rattling during the Spanish Civil War compelled the Committee of Imperial Defence to reevaluate the question as to whether or not fighter squadrons should be based on Malta. The RAF refused to send any new fighter aircraft to Malta, claiming that all were needed in England in an effort to maintain parity with the ever-expanding Luftwaffe. The RAF did recommend the construction of a new concrete airfield at Luqa to the south of Valletta, which began in 1939, and the conversion of the civilian aerodrome at Takali in the centre of the island into a military airfield in the event of war. If aircraft were to operate from the island in wartime, the additional airfields would allow for a stronger force to be based there and allow greater dispersal in the event of air attack.

Without a strong fighter presence from the RAF, the Royal Navy believed that the best protection for its ships and facilities on Malta lay in a strong network of anti-aircraft gun batteries. In 1935 when the Mediterranean Fleet sailed to Alexandria, Malta only had eight QF 3in 20cwt anti-aircraft guns, dating from World War I, on the island. For the next four years the Royal Navy pushed for more anti-aircraft guns for the island, receiving a handful of heavy guns and several light guns, but nearly all new guns were going to air defences in Great Britain. With conflict increasingly imminent in the summer of 1939, the Committee of Imperial Defence agreed to a naval proposal for Malta's aerial defence, referred to as the CID Scale B defence plan, which consisted of 112 heavy anti-aircraft guns and 60 light anti-aircraft guns, a scheme to be completed by April 1941. Navy analysts calculated that the anti-aircraft arrangement outlined in the Scale B plan, once fully established and operational, would inflict around 25 per cent casualties on an attacking enemy force, a high enough casualty rate to severely damage the morale of Italian airmen and to dissuade the Regia Aeronautica from continuing its attacks.

Allied defeats in Western Europe during the spring of 1940, however, compelled RAF Fighter Command in England to keep as many anti-aircraft guns in the British Isles as it could, but Malta's air defence had improved somewhat by June 1940. In terms of heavy anti-aircraft guns there were 16 QF 3in 20cwt guns (22,000ft ceiling), eight QF 3.7in guns (30,000ft ceiling), and ten QF 4.5in Mk II guns (41,000ft ceiling). Light anti-aircraft

40mm Bofors gun position overlooking the Grand Harbour on Malta. (Imperial War Museum GM 946)

armament consisted of eight 40mm Bofors guns, several QF 2-pdr pom-poms taken from naval vessels, and a number of machine guns. In addition there were 24 searchlights. The anti-aircraft guns were concentrated around Valletta, the dockyard, and Marsaxlokk Bay; with only so many guns available at the time it seemed prudent to position them around the areas most likely to be targeted by the Regia Aeronautica.

As no RAF or FAA squadrons were yet based on the island, the anti-aircraft batteries planned for the airfields would have to wait until more guns arrived. Perhaps the most remarkable and valuable component of Malta's air defence was the Air Ministry Experimental Station (AMES) 241, the first mobile radar system located outside of Great Britain. It was set up in January 1939 on the Dingli Cliffs, the highest point on the island, and could detect incoming aircraft up to 50 miles away.

The CID's Scale B plan had also called for four RAF fighter squadrons to be based on Malta for aerial defence by the end of 1940 but the success of the German blitzkrieg in the West that spring drove RAF Fighter Command to harbour all Hurricane and Spitfire units in the British Isles. The Royal Navy felt that the complete measures of Scale B would have created a strong enough air defence to keep part of the Mediterranean Fleet at Malta during wartime, but as it was nowhere near finished and there was no fighter cover for the dockyard, it retired to Alexandria once Mussolini's intentions became apparent. But there too it begged for fighter cover and received only five Hurricanes from England in June.

Malta did receive a handful of fighters from an unexpected source in that April however. In early 1940, the aircraft carrier HMS *Glorious* took up station in the Mediterranean and put ashore 18 crated Gloster Sea Gladiator biplane fighters at RAF Kalafrana seaplane base as a reserve for 802 Naval Air Squadron which was embarked aboard her. When *Glorious* was transferred to Norway to cover the British landings at Narvik in April, 12 of these Gladiators were left behind at Kalafrana. The Air Officer Commanding on Malta, Air Commodore F.H.M. Maynard, asked the Royal Navy's Commander-in-Chief, Mediterranean, Vice-Admiral Andrew Cunningham if these fighters could be used to form an air defence unit, a request which was granted. On 19 April, four of the crated Sea Gladiators were assembled, along with another two in early May; the remaining six were to be cannibalized for spare parts. These six aircraft formed the Hal Far Fighter Flight. The only pilots available on the island were a handful of volunteers, raised from Fairey Swordfish floatplane pilots from No. 3 Anti-Aircraft Co-operation Unit stationed at Kalafrana and several staff officers assigned to Hal Far and Luqa. Having no prior fighter experience, these pilots took it upon themselves to learn fighter tactics and had almost two months to train on the Sea Gladiators prior to the first Italian air attacks on the island.

The Sea Gladiator was the aircraft carrier variant of the Gloster Gladiator biplane fighter. The Gladiator was a refinement of the company's earlier Gauntlet fighter, equipped with a more powerful engine and possessing a maximum speed of 253mph. Unlike its predecessor it was equipped with four .303in machine guns and was the first British production fighter equipped with an enclosed cockpit. Having first flown in September 1934, it initially appeared unlikely that the Gladiator would enter RAF service, as the first generation of British monoplane fighters was just beginning development. However, the Abyssinian Crisis highlighted the RAF's need for new fighter aircraft and compelled it to put the Gladiator into production as an interim fighter until the new monoplanes could enter service; this was a circumstance the Gladiator shared with the CR.42, but unlike its Italian rival it was not kept in production past 1940. Due to the small number of operational Sea Gladiators at any one time on Malta, Regia Aeronautica fighters only rarely encountered them.

Although not present on the island when Italy declared war, the Hawker Hurricane became the primary RAF fighter on Malta from the summer of 1940 until the spring of 1942. The Hurricane was the RAF's first monoplane fighter and first flew in November 1935, entering service in December 1937. The Hurricane was generally outclassed by the slightly newer Spitfire as well as the Bf 109, but it was the RAF's most numerous fighter by the summer of 1940. While RAF Fighter Command in Great Britain was reluctant to part with any modern fighters in the wake of the Allied disaster in France, the Italian entry into the war compelled the release of a handful of Hurricanes to the Mediterranean theatre. It was believed that the Hurricane Mk I could hold its own against the more lightly armed fighters of the Regia Aeronautica.

CAMPAIGN OBJECTIVES

Invasion or neutralization

Italian heavy cruisers sailing in formation in the Bay of Naples during a Regia Marina fleet review in May 1938. Largely developed as a fleet-in-being, the Regia Marina had only one regiment of Marines at the beginning of the war and little amphibious capability. (Hugo Jaeger/Timepix/ The LIFE Picture Collection/Getty Images)

In mid-April 1940 Mussolini issued the Comando Supremo with the following general directives:

> To prepare for military intervention on the side of Germany including:
> 1.) air and naval offensive operations against Allied naval and maritime units in the Mediterranean
> 2.) maintain a defensive stance against France and in Libya and East Africa
> 3.) remain neutral towards but look for convenient offensive opportunities against Yugoslavia and Greece.

No exact date for entry into the war was given pending the success of the coming German offensive against France. Pricolo was shocked, particularly as only four months earlier he had shown Mussolini in detail how poor the state of the Regia Aeronautica was. He argued that as the Regia Aeronautica had to operate within the full 2,300-mile length of the Mediterranean and points beyond, its limited resources and aircraft would be stretched too thin. This would not allow for a proper concentration of force for any decisive independent air campaign. German aerial successes stemmed from having a significantly larger air force and having a smaller theatre of operations. However on 29 May, after witnessing the rapid German victories in Scandinavia and Western Europe, Mussolini instructed his generals and admirals to be prepared for military action by 5 June; he felt that if Italian entry was delayed any longer, there would be no seat for Italy at a German redrawing of Europe's borders. Mussolini's opportunistic strategy for Italian dominance in the Mediterranean basin is best summarized in his own words to General Pietro Badoglio, *Capo di Stato Maggiore Generale* or Chief of Staff of the Armed Forces, on 26 May 1940: 'I assure you the war will be over in September, and that I need a few thousand dead so as to be able to attend the peace conference as a belligerent.' With the British Expeditionary Force beginning its evacuation at Dunkirk, Pricolo, and Italy's other military commanders, decided to accept Mussolini's optimistic assessment of the course of the war. On 5 June, the armed forces were informed that Italy would commence hostilities against Britain and France five days later on 10 June.

On 29 May Commando Supremo put into motion *Piano di radunata 12* (P.R.12), or Joint Plan 12, a joint forces mobilization plan developed between 1938 and 1940 for a scenario preparing for war with Britain and France and possible hostilities with Yugoslavia, Greece, and Turkey. To this end the combat strength of Regia Aeronautica was distributed across the entire Mediterranean basin and organized with the following objectives in mind:

UNIT	STRENGTH	AREA OF OPERATIONS
1a Squadra Aerea	12× bomber Gruppi 7× fighter Gruppi	Based in the Po Valley for operations along the French border
2a Squadra Aerea	11× bomber Gruppi 3× fighter Gruppi	Based on Sicily for operations against Malta, North Africa, and the Central Mediterranean
3a Squadra Aerea	6× bomber Gruppi 1× assault Gruppo 4× fighter Gruppo	Based in Tuscany for operations against Metropolitian France and Corsica
4a Zona Aerea e Aeronautica Albania	6× bomber Gruppi 2× fighter Gruppi	Based in Puglia for operations against Yugoslavia, Greece, the Adriatic, and the Central Mediterranean.
Aeronautica della Sardegna	6× bomber Gruppi 1× assault Gruppo 1× fighter Gruppo	Based on Sardinia for operations against North Africa, the Western Mediterranean, and the French Mediterranean coast.
Aeronautica della Libia	8× bomber Gruppi 2× assault Gruppi 3× fighter Gruppi	Based in Libya for operations against Egypt, Tunisia, and the Central and Eastern Mediterranean.
Aeronautica dell'Egeo-Rodi	2× bomber Gruppi 1× fighter Squadriglia	Based on Italy's Aegean islands for operations against the Middle East and the Eastern Mediterranean.

Fortunately for the Regia Aeronautica, P.R.12 was largely defensive in nature with only the navy and air force expected to undertake limited offensive operations against British and French targets in the Mediterranean. Given the rapid course of the campaign in France in late May and early June, both the Regia Marina and Regia Aeronautica were reluctant to waste precious resources on limited offensive operations in a war that was likely to be decided in a few weeks. Only Malta, with its proximity to the Italian sea lanes to North Africa and ability to base offensive naval and air units, appeared to pose a potential threat to Italy's internal lines of supply in the Central Mediterranean. For this reason Commando Supremo was eager to have the Regia Marina and Regia Aeronautica neutralize Malta's offensive capabilities from the outset of hostilities.

Prudent military planning demanded the neutralization and/or occupation of such a potentially dangerous enemy base as Malta. Since the Abyssinian Crisis the Regia Marina conducted several studies weighing the merits of an amphibious assault on Malta. Even with the British Mediterranean Fleet now based in Alexandria, the Royal Navy could still base light surface units and submarines at Malta while the island's airfields and seaplane bases could accommodate a large number of aircraft. The most detailed pre-war naval study for an assault on Malta, *Documento di Guerra* D.G. 10/A2, was drafted in December 1938 and called for an assault force of 40,000 army troops, offloaded by 80 shallow-draught vessels, and supported by the bulk of the Regia Marina's surface vessels and at least 500 aircraft. The study did not give any further specific details regarding the types of units required for such an amphibious operation, and neither did it contain any operational insight from the army or the air force. The lack of inter-service coordination had not improved since the Abyssinian Crisis and Admiral Cavagnari continued to be unwilling to commit the Regia Marina to any campaign that might diminish the strength of his battle fleet. Due to the rigid independence of the armed services, Cavagnari assumed that the Regia Aeronautica would counter any enemy aerial threat to the battle fleet or to Italian sea lanes as the neutralization of enemy air power was a role to be assumed by the air force; thus he believed there was little need for proactive coordination with the Regia Aeronautica. Aware of the Regia Aeronautica's continued lack of success in bombing exercises against his ships, he assumed that enemy air forces faced the same problems and completely disregarded any threat from aerial bombing. In his mind the only need the navy had for aircraft was for reconnaissance, anti-submarine patrol, and gunnery spotting. If the Regia Aeronautica wanted to further develop aerial anti-shipping capabilities, it was the air force's own prerogative and it alone should bear the expense of development and equipping itself.

Targets

With amphibious invasion off the table, this left aerial neutralization as the only means to eliminate any British offensive operations from Malta. As the Regia Aeronautica had not collaborated in the Regia Marina's previous invasion studies, it had no plans involving the other armed services with relation to Malta, and neither was it called on to submit any. Its only expectation was to neutralize the island's offensive capabilities. To this end the 2a Squadra Aerea in Sicily was ordered to attack Malta's naval and aerial infrastructure. Pre-war aerial surveys and intelligence gathering revealed the areas to be targeted for aerial bombardment. Royal Navy ships relied upon the naval facilities in the area around Malta's Grand Harbour and Marsamxett Harbour, consisting of six graving docks, extensive workshops, underground arsenals, two torpedo depots, and 16 oil and petrol storage depots. A particularly inviting target was the 60,000-ton-lift-capacity Admiralty Floating Dock 8, capable of servicing most British capital ships and anchored in the Grand Harbour. Manoel Island in Marsamxett Harbour housed the docking and service facilities for the Mediterranean Fleet's submarines. A number of forts and fortresses were located in and around the Valletta area and were used to house coastal artillery batteries, barracks, ammunition stores, and some anti-aircraft batteries. Marsaxlokk Bay on the eastern side of the island possessed naval facilities, including a torpedo depot and seven oil and petrol storage depots, for smaller vessels as well as a seaplane base at Kalafrana. Finally there was the military airfield at Hal Far where it was believed an RAF squadron or two were based.

A large bombardment would be carried out on the first day of hostilities, with subsequent raids pending the success of the first and the actions of the British. As anti-aircraft fire was expected over Malta's military targets, an attack altitude of 12,000 to 18,000ft was recommended as it was calculated to be high enough to avoid most British anti-aircraft fire. Fighters were to escort the bombers during these initial bombardment missions as aerial reconnaissance suggested the presence of 12 British fighters on the island. Any British aircraft not destroyed on the ground in the bombardment or in the air by fighter escorts would be destroyed in subsequent fighter sweeps over the island if deemed necessary.

To conserve ordnance a sustained aerial bombardment was not planned at the

High-altitude Regia Aeronautica reconnaissance photograph of Malta showing the Royal Navy's various facilities around the Grand Harbour in the centre of the photo and the submarine base on Manoel Island in the centre bottom of the photo. The seaplane base at Kalafrana is located on the right-centre rim of Marsaxlokk Bay (top centre) while Hal Far is just to its right in the photo. (Archivio centrale dello Stato 11619)

outset, as 2a Squadra Aerea also had to be able to react to potential French aerial operations launched from Corsica and Metropolitan France as well as any Anglo-French naval activity in the Central Mediterranean. Against its 1,796 operational combat aircraft, the Regia Aeronautica calculated that the French had 1,040 operational combat aircraft spread around the Mediterranean, augmented by 1,020 based in Metropolitan France, and that the British had 620 operational combat aircraft spread throughout the Mediterranean. This was a gross overestimation: the French had only 152 fighters and 191 bombers in the Western Mediterranean and southern France while the British had only 75 fighters and 96 bombers based around the entire Mediterranean. Thus the Regia Aeronautica believed it was about to enter a conflict outnumbered by 3-to-2 when instead it outnumbered the Allies by 3.5-to-1. This intelligence failure handicapped the Regia Aeronautica from taking opportune aggressive action at the outset of the conflict. This observation aside, Pricolo and the Regia Aeronautica leadership felt that a limited deployment of the equipment and capabilities of the 2a Squadra Aerea was sufficient to neutralize Malta's aerial and naval infrastructure until the anticipated cessation of hostilities. With a negotiated peace with Britain only a few months away, Pricolo calculated that this would be enough of an effort to achieve the expectations of Comando Supremo with regards to Malta and to validate the Regia Aeronautica's long-held claims about victory through air power.

ORDER OF BATTLE: 11 JUNE 1940

REGIA AERONAUTICA

2A SQUADRA AEREA (PALERMO)
Generale Di Squadra Aerea Gennaro Tedeschini Lalli
1a Divisione Aerea Aquila (Palermo) – Generale di Divisione Aerea Vincenzo Velardi
1° Stormo C.T. (Trapani) – Tenente Colonnello Mario Piccinini
17° Gruppo (Palermo) – Maggiore Bruno Brambilla (23 CR.42)
157° Gruppo (Trapani) – Maggiore Guido Nobili (19 CR.42)
6° Gruppo autonomo C.T. (Catania) – Tenente Colonnello Armando François (26 C.200)

3a Divisione Aerea Centauro (Catania) – Generale di Divisione Aerea Ettore Lodi
11° Stormo B.T. (Comiso) – Colonnello Arnaldo Lubelli (33 SM.79)
33° Gruppo – Tenente Colonnello Ferzi Forte
34° Gruppo – Tenente Colonnello Vittorio Cannaviello
34° Stormo B.T. (Catania) – Colonnello Umberto Mazzini (33 SM.79)
52° Gruppo – Maggiore Paolo Maiorca
53° Gruppo – Tenente Colonnello Luigi Rossetti
41° Stormo B.T. (Gela) – Colonnello Enrico Pezzi (18 SM.79)
59° Gruppo – Tenente Colonnello Emilio Draghelli
60° Gruppo – Tenente Colonnello Pasquale d'Ippolito

11a Brigata Aerea Nibbio (Castelvetrano)
30° Stormo B.T. (Sciacca) – Colonnello Antonio Serra (26 SM.79)
87° Gruppo – Tenente Colonnello Vincenzo Tabacchini
90° Gruppo – Tenente Colonnello Gennaro La Manna
36° Stormo B.T. (Castelvetrano) – Colonnello Carlo Drago (32 SM.79)
108° Gruppo – Tenente Colonnello Virgilio Silvestri
109° Gruppo – Tenente Colonnello Ugo Vincenzi
96° Gruppo autonomo B.a.T. (Pantelleria) – Capitano Ercolano Ercolani (11 SM.85)

ROYAL AIR FORCE

Air Officer Commanding, Malta: Air Commodore F.H.M. Maynard
Fighter Flight (Hal Far) Sqn Ldr A.C. Martin (6 Gloster Sea Gladiator)

THE 1940 CAMPAIGN
Italy's first strikes

CR.42s of 73a and 96a Squadriglie of 9° Gruppo C.T. over the Mediterranean. (courtesy of Douglas Dildy)

In the early morning of 11 June, 55 Savoia-Marchetti SM.79s and 18 Macchi C.200 escorts undertook the first bombing raids against Malta, hitting Hal Far airfield, the seaplane base at Kalafrana, and the dockyards around Valletta. The bombers conducted their attacks at 15,000ft, dropping a total of 30 250kg and 112 100kg bombs. After assessing reconnaissance photos taken after the morning's raids, 2a Squadra Aerea dispatched a further raid in the afternoon by 38 SM.79s from the same Stormi. Five bombers hit Valletta while the other 33 attacked Hal Far and Kalfrana, all bombing from 15,000ft. The SM.79s had no fighter escort on this raid but there was no response from the Gladiators at Hal Far; all of the attackers returned safely to their bases after dropping 15 250kg, 204 100kg bombs, and 20 20kg incendiary bombs. These two raids were to be the largest undertaken against Malta by the Regia Aeronautica for months. That being said, the results were to serve as an ominous portent regarding the Regia Aeronautica's operational effectiveness. Despite over 43,000kg (nearly 48 tons) of bombs being dropped on 11 June, little damage was done to Malta's military infrastructure. Some 250kg bombs were dropped on Hal Far airfield but not enough to do serious damage. The bomb craters from the raid were quickly filled in and the only materiel damaged was a few buses and cars. There was no damage to Malta's naval facilities either.

For the next two weeks, Regia Aeronautica SM.79s conducted several small nuisance raids against Malta, attacking in small groups usually of five to ten bombers, or attacking singly at regular intervals from the same high altitudes. While minimal damage was done overall, a bomb from a single SM.79 raid on the night of 20/21 June hit the floating dock at the dockyard, breaking its back and putting it out of service. The Regia Aeronautica considered this to be a strategic objective achieved, limiting Malta's naval offensive capabilities. Raids on 22 and 23 June saw the first Regia Aeronautica losses to Malta's defenders. A Gladiator intercepted and shot down an SM.79 of 34° Stormo on

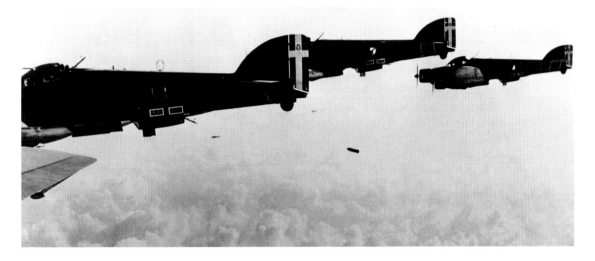

a reconnaissance mission on the afternoon of the 22nd. In the early afternoon of the following day 15 SM.79s of 11° Stormo B.T., escorted by C.200s of 6° Gruppo Autonomo C.T., raided Valletta and Luqa and were intercepted by two Gladiators. One of the C.200s was shot down in a brief dogfight, becoming the first Italian fighter loss of the campaign. Following the heavy raids of 11 June, the majority of 2a Squadra Aerea's combat operations were against French targets until the Armistice of Villa Incisa between Italy and France came into effect on 25 June. With France out of the war, Generale di Squadra Aerea Gennaro Tedeschini Lalli, commander of 2a Squadra Aerea, was ordered to devote the full weight of his bomber units to the sterilization of Malta's military infrastructure and impose a state of aerial denial upon the RAF on the island. To begin this objective Lalli unleashed 25 SM.79s against Hal Far and Valletta on 26 June and conducted another smaller raid on 28 June.

The bomb bay of the SM.79 was smaller than that of other Italian medium bombers and its internal bomb racks were mounted vertically inside the bomb bay. As the tail of the bomb dropped first the heavier nose flipped around and caused the entire bomb to wobble in freefall, thus affecting the SM.79s' bombing accuracy. (ullstein bild via Getty Images)

The Hurricanes arrive

The end of Italy's first month in the war brought a setback, however. The first was the arrival of five Hawker Hurricanes on 21–22 June for operations at Hal Far. While these aircraft could not be counted as substantial reinforcements, they gave the defenders a faster and better-armed fighter than the Gladiator. The second setback was more grievous and stemmed directly from the lack of proper training exercised by the Regia Aeronautica. As mentioned previously Regia Aeronautica fighter pilots preferred and relied on tried-and-tested turning dogfights, particularly as many fighter units were being re-equipped with the new CR.42 biplane. When putting the G.50 and C.200 monoplanes into tight manoeuvres however, pilots found that the aircraft could roll spontaneously in either direction when approaching a stall, resulting in a violent spin, or autorotation. Two C.200s crashed in March and May of 1940 due to autorotation and pilots feared to put the aircraft into any serious manoeuvres. The Regia Aeronautica's *Direzione Superiore Studi ed Esperienze* (DSSE), or Directorate of Advanced Studies and Experiments, were aware of the threat of autorotation in monoplanes before the war but its instructional departments made little effort to amend pilot training as a result. Due to increasing pilot trepidation the Regia Aeronautica grounded its C.200s at the end of June 1940 and even considered halting production. Cooler heads eventually prevailed as Macchi designers added a detachable wing leading edge to the aircraft that, with modified flying instruction, largely corrected the problem. Nevertheless the C.200s were out of service for much of the summer as they were modified, a process which was not completed until October. C.200 pilots had to adjust to monoplane dive-and-climb tactics over time,

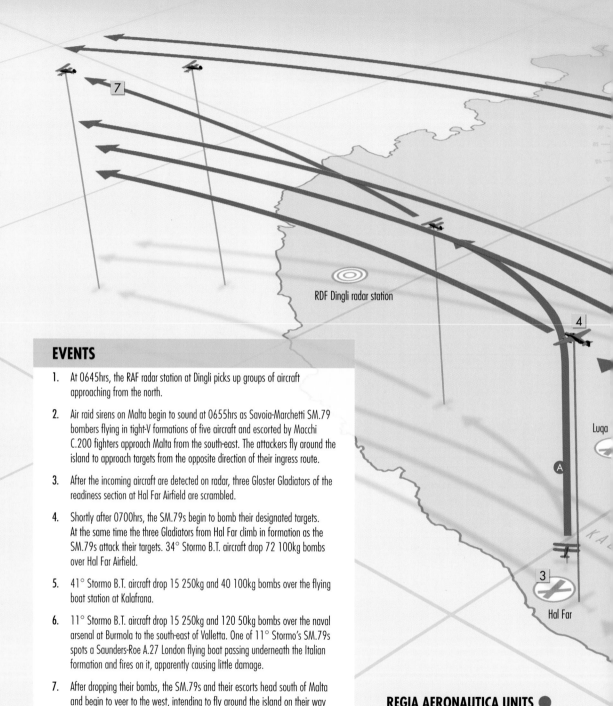

RDF Dingli radar station

Luqa

KAL

Hal Far

EVENTS

1. At 0645hrs, the RAF radar station at Dingli picks up groups of aircraft approaching from the north.

2. Air raid sirens on Malta begin to sound at 0655hrs as Savoia-Marchetti SM.79 bombers flying in tight-V formations of five aircraft and escorted by Macchi C.200 fighters approach Malta from the south-east. The attackers fly around the island to approach targets from the opposite direction of their ingress route.

3. After the incoming aircraft are detected on radar, three Gloster Gladiators of the readiness section at Hal Far Airfield are scrambled.

4. Shortly after 0700hrs, the SM.79s begin to bomb their designated targets. At the same time the three Gladiators from Hal Far climb in formation as the SM.79s attack their targets. 34° Stormo B.T. aircraft drop 72 100kg bombs over Hal Far Airfield.

5. 41° Stormo B.T. aircraft drop 15 250kg and 40 100kg bombs over the flying boat station at Kalafrana.

6. 11° Stormo B.T. aircraft drop 15 250kg and 120 50kg bombs over the naval arsenal at Burmola to the south-east of Valletta. One of 11° Stormo's SM.79s spots a Saunders-Roe A.27 London flying boat passing underneath the Italian formation and fires on it, apparently causing little damage.

7. After dropping their bombs, the SM.79s and their escorts head south of Malta and begin to veer to the west, intending to fly around the island on their way back to Sicily in order to avoid anti-aircraft fire. At this time, the Gladiators reach the altitude of the attackers. Two of the biplanes go after one of the SM.79 formations that attacked Hal Far, peppering a bomber with bullets but with no serious damage. The other Gladiator attacks an SM.79 formation that struck Burmola but is engaged by one of the escorting C.200s. After a twisting dogfight both fighters hit each other but neither is seriously damaged. Eventually the attackers use their superior speed to escape with no losses. The defenders return to Hal Far, also without loss. The attack is over by 0725hrs.

REGIA AERONAUTICA UNITS ●

1. 30 SM.79s of 34° Stormo B.T.
2. 10 SM.79s of 41° Stormo B.T.
3. 9 C.200s of 79a Squadriglia
4. 15 SM.79s of 11° Stormo B.T.
5. 9 C.200s of 88a Squadriglia

ROYAL AIR FORCE UNITS ●

A. Fighter Flight (Hal Far)

The first aerial bombardment of Malta

11 June 1940

ALTITUDES

▬	15,000ft
▬	10,000–15,000ft

KEY

Airfield

Radar station

Seaplane base

VALETTA

GRAND HARBOUR

MARSAXLOKK

Kalafrana seaplane base

MARSAXLOKK BAY

5

6

1

2

2

2

3

4

CR.42s escorting a SM.79 bombardment mission over Malta in August 1940. (Archivio centrale dello Stato 04208)

taking away the numerical advantage in monoplane fighters held by the Regia Aeronautica over Malta early in the campaign. To replace the grounded C.200s of 6° Gruppo autonomo C.T., the 32 CR.42 fighters of 9° Gruppo C.T. were transferred to Comiso on 1 July. This Gruppo was transferred to North Africa on 15 July and was replaced the following day by the 29 CR.42s of 23° Gruppo C.T.

On the morning of 3 July, two SM.79s of 109° Gruppo B.T. flew a reconnaissance over Malta, escorted by nine CR.42s of 9° Gruppo C.T. On this mission one of the CR.42s shot down a single Hurricane which had flown up, becoming the first Italian fighter kill over Malta. Thirty SM.79s raided Valletta, Hal Far, and Takali on the afternoon of 6 July and ten SM.79s hit the dockyard the following day. On 10 July, 20 SM.79s from 87° and 90° Gruppi B.T. attacked the dockyard and the submarine facilities on Manoel Island but were fiercely attacked by three Hurricanes, resulting in the loss of one bomber and damage to over half the force. Twenty-one CR.42s of 9° Gruppo C.T. were supposed to have escorted the bombers during their attack but arrived at the rendezvous point almost an hour before the bombers and were forced to return to base, low on fuel. The fighters were unaware of the delayed departure of the bombers because the CR.42 was not equipped with a radio, a cost-saving omission shared by most other Regia Aeronautica fighters at this time; this would have serious tactical ramifications for the Regia Aeronautica's fighter arm. The next combat over the island occurred when 12 CR.42s of 23° Gruppo C.T. flew a visual reconnaissance mission on the morning of 16 July and were intercepted by a Hurricane and a Gladiator. The Hurricane was shot down but a CR.42 was lost as well.

First fighter sweeps

The Regia Aeronautica suffered another setback on the morning of 2 August when 12 more Hurricanes landed at Luqa. These reinforcements were embarked upon the aircraft carrier HMS *Argus* in Great Britain and sailed to a point in the western Mediterranean from where they could fly off and reach Malta. This method of delivery was to become the standard way of sending fighter reinforcements to the island during the campaign due to the lack of a suitable overland route. On 6 August these Hurricanes were merged with the Gladiators and Hurricanes already on the island to form No. 261 Squadron. Aware of the arrival of the reinforcements, 2a Squadra Aerea's fighter units attempted a new tactic to whittle down Malta's fighters, sending a fighter sweep of 17 CR.42s on 4 August and another sweep of 20 CR.42s the following day. On both missions the biplane fighters approached the island at around 20,000ft. The intention was for the large group of Italian fighters to dive and overwhelm any defending fighters attempting to climb up to intercept. On each occasion two Hurricanes were scrambled after the approaching Italian force was detected on radar but by this time RAF fighter pilots had learned to climb towards the south, away from an attacking force; this allowed more time for RAF fighters to climb to the attackers' altitude in an attempt to minimize the possibility of being ambushed from above. During these fighter sweeps the Hurricanes did not engage the Italian fighters, observing from a distance.

Due to the superior maneuverability of the CR.42, Hurricane pilots on Malta had been instructed to avoid unnecessary encounters with the biplane fighters when heavily outnumbered and to avoid engaging in turning fights; attacks on the biplanes should be made using dive-and-climb attacks, taking advantage of the Hurricane's superior speed. On both occasions the CR.42s retired to their bases, frustrated by the seeming lack of enemy response but still not completely aware of the early warning advantage of radar. 2a Squadra Aerea continued its sporadic bombing raids over the island over the course of August as well. An early afternoon raid on Hal Far on 18 August by ten SM.79s and 19 CR.42s is notable as it resulted in the first British aircraft destroyed on the ground on Malta – a Swordfish torpedo bomber. Another raid against Hal Far and Luqa two days later by six SM.79s and 16 CR.42s managed to destroy a Blenheim bomber, on its way from England to Egypt, on the ground. A Hurricane was shot down on 18 August while a CR.42 was lost in a light raid on Hal Far on 24 August.

Italy's Stukas

In the early evening of 5 September the Regia Aeronautica launched its first dive-bombing precision strikes against the island. Six Junkers Ju 87s of 96° Gruppo Bombardamento a Tuffo took off from Comiso, escorted by CR.42s from 23° Gruppo and C.200s from 6° Gruppo – the first modified C.200s to return to Sicily following the type's grounding in late June – and attacked ground installations around the south-eastern end of the island. The British, unaware of the Italian acquisition of the Ju 87, initially believed that the raid was carried out by the Luftwaffe and feared the arrival of German squadrons in the theatre. Fortunately for the RAF, this was not the case: the Regia Aeronautica only had a total of 15 operational Ju 87s at that time.

The Regia Aeronautica's first dive-bomber unit, 96° Gruppo B.a.T., had been formed on 29 May 1940, with 18 Savoia-Marchetti SM.85s and the prototype SM.86. Shortly after its formation the unit was transferred to the island of Pantelleria for anticipated action against Malta. The humid conditions on the island caused problems maintaining the wood-and-fabric aircraft. After only a handful of reconnaissance missions with the aircraft in

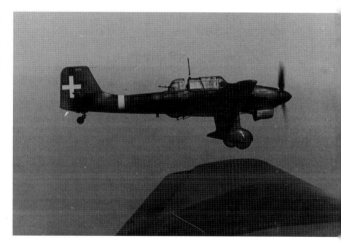

Regia Aeronautica Ju 87 Picchiatelli over the Mediterranean. (Archivio centrale dello Stato 15461)

9° Gruppo strafing attack on Hal Far, 4 July 1940

At 05:00 on the morning of 4 July 1940, 24 Fiat CR.42s of 9° Gruppo took off from Comiso to undertake a strafing mission over Hal Far airfield. Shortly before 06:00 the attackers arrived over Hal Far and spotted four Hurricanes, two Gladiators, and several Swordfish on the ground, spread out around the runway. No enemy fighters were in the air over the island and the attack proceeded without RAF interference. Six of the CR.42s dived to the deck and swept over the airfield at 30ft, firing at the aircraft and vehicles around the airfield. Nine CR.42s patrolled overhead at 1,000ft while the remaining nine provided top cover high above. After several passes the attackers returned to Sicily, claiming to have destroyed one bomber and seven fighters on the ground. Most of the CR.42s took fire from the anti-aircraft batteries around the airfield, some requiring a lengthy period of repair. In reality only two Swordfish were slightly damaged in the strafing attack, a poor return for the amount of damage sustained by the attackers. Groups of both CR.42 and Macchi C.200 fighters conducted strafing attacks on Malta's airfields throughout 1940 and 1941 but these attacks rarely resulted in any significant damage to targets on the ground. This was largely due to the relatively weak armament of both fighters: only two 12.7mm Breda SAFAT machine guns. This was also a disadvantage in combat with more heavily armed Hurricanes. A lack of dedicated fighter-bombers and ground-attack aircraft forced the Regia Aeronautica to employ its lightly-armed fighters in strafing missions throughout the campaign.

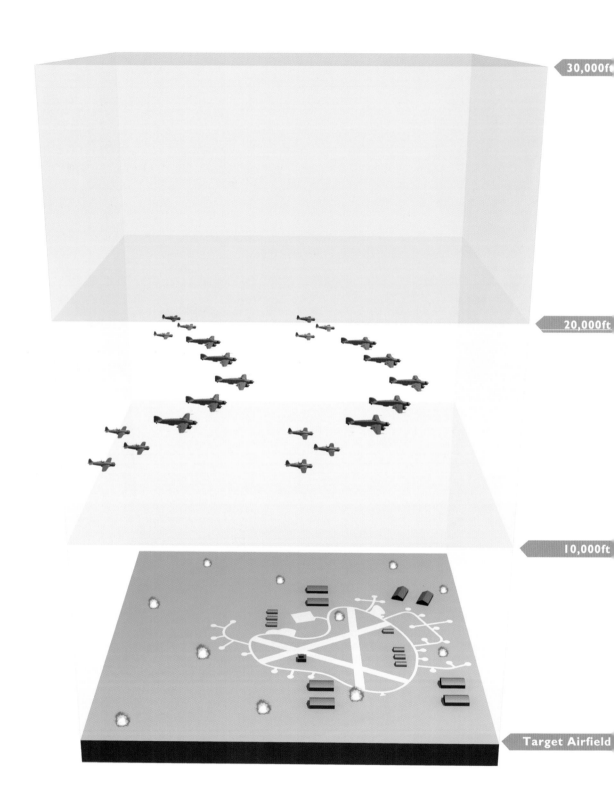

30,000ft

20,000ft

10,000ft

Target Airfield

OPPOSITE REGIA AERONAUTICA DAYLIGHT BOMBING TACTICS

During daylight operations Italian bombers, in groups of three or five (one or two *sezione* of a *squadriglia*), flew in a 'V' formation and approached their target typically around 15,000ft. Escorting fighters flew close by on each side of the bomber formation at the same altitude. The close escort resulted in a tactical disadvantage as the accompanying fighters were unable to dive on attackers that approached the bombers at or above their ingress altitude. Pre-war training dictated that medium bombers conduct horizontal bombing attacks from higher altitudes in order to minimize the threat posed by anti-aircraft fire. While better protecting the bombers this tactic resulted in poor bombing accuracy, particularly given the limitation of the Jozza U.2/U.3 aiming device, a pre-war manual vector bombsight that lacked the gyroscopic stabilization of newer tachometric bombsights. Wind and greater freefall distance to the target resulted in a very wide bomb spread across the target area and beyond. The effectiveness of Italian bombs further limited the Regia Aeronautica's ability to effectively attack Malta's airfields. At the beginning of the war the Regia Aeronautica's aerial ordnance stocks were primarily made up of 100kg and smaller bombs. These smaller bombs could do little effective damage to the hard and rocky soil that made up Malta's airfields and Italian bombs also suffered from a relatively high rate of duds. With the exception of the raids on 11 June 1940, Regia Aeronautica attacks rarely amounted to more than five to ten bombers, on an increasingly irregular basis – simply not the attack volume necessary to keep Malta's airfields out of action.

June and July, 96° Gruppo's pilots compelled the Regia Aeronautica to remove the SM.85 from combat, claiming that operational use would eventually result in a 100 per cent loss rate. Aware of the serious problems with the SM.85, on 22 June General Pricolo began a series of direct negotiations with his German counterpart, Reichsmarschall Hermann Göring, which eventually resulted in the purchase of 50 Junkers Ju 87s from Luftwaffe stocks on 4 July. Eleven days later, on 15 July, the 15 pilots of 96° Gruppo B.a.T. were sent to the Luftwaffe's *Stukaschule 2* in Graz to learn how to operate the Ju 87 dive bomber. With the Ju 87, the Regia Aeronautica finally had an aircraft that could hit pinpoint targets, namely hangars, runways, and even individual aircraft around Malta's airfields. The Ju 87 *Picchiatelli* returned to Malta on 15 September when 12 of them, plus the prototype of the Savoia-Marchetti SM.86 dive bomber, and escorted by 18 CR.42s from 23° Gruppo C.T. and six C.200s from 6° Gruppo C.T., attacked Hal Far that morning. No serious damage was inflicted on this raid but the dive bombers returned again two days later. Twelve Ju 87s, with top cover provided by six C.200s and 21 CR.42s from 6° and 23° Gruppi C.T. respectively, attacked Luqa and destroyed a Wellington bomber on the ground as well as damaging several hangars. Four Hurricanes were up and shot down a Ju 87.

Withdrawal and reversals

96° Gruppo B.a.T. did not operate for long over Malta; the unit transferred to Lecce on mainland Italy on 27 September. At the same time the Regia Aeronautica scaled back its operations over Malta and only a handful of missions were flown over the island from late September until the end of October. Only one bombing raid was conducted against the airfields during that period, on 27 September, when six SM.79s hit Hal Far and Luqa and destroyed one Hurricane on the ground. Most 2a Squadra Aerea missions over Malta were now reconnaissance flights. The reason for the lack of Regia Aeronautica activity was that nearly all of the SM.79 units on Sicily had been transferred off the island over the course of the autumn; by the end of November the SM.79s of 87° and 90° Gruppi B.T. were the only medium bombers left under 2° Squadra Aerea command. Some of the bomber units were sent to North Africa to assist with the Italian campaign in Egypt which began on 9 September. Others were transferred to Albania and southern Italy due to Mussolini's abrupt decision to invade Greece on 28 October – a jealous overreaction to the stationing of German troops in Romania for protection against the Soviet Union.

C.200s of 6° Gruppo autonomo C.T. taking off from Catania. Note the cockpit canopies on these early model C.200s. (Archivio centrale dello Stato 04087)

General Lalli did not protest the transfer of the majority of his bomber units to the new North African and Greek fronts. Although Malta had not capitulated he felt that his aircraft had successfully neutralized the island's aerial and naval offensive capabilities. He claimed that the lack of RAF offensive action as well as the absence of Royal Navy vessels was proof that the 2a Squadra Aerea's mission over Malta had been achieved. Furthermore the fact that Italian convoys to North Africa were arriving safely with minimal interference seemed to suggest that the British were unwilling to contest control of the central Mediterranean sea lanes. Without intelligence to suggest the contrary, it appeared to Lalli as if his forces had enforced a state of aerial denial upon the RAF forces on Malta. This conclusion was drawn already in August and explains the decrease in Regia Aeronautica activity over the island from that point on. The RAF had done little to reinforce the island with the exception of several Hurricane fighters. An advocate of Douhetian theory, Lalli was reluctant to question the perceived results of his bombardment campaign, as was the Douhetian leadership of the Regia Aeronautica.

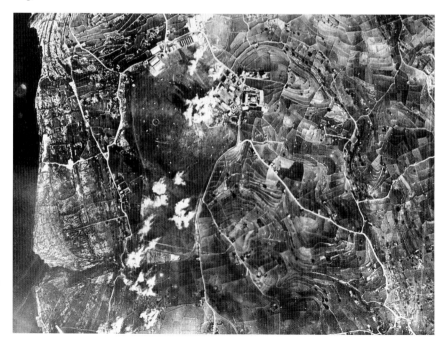

Hal Far under attack, photographed during a Regia Aeronautica bombardment. Italian bombardments against Malta's airfields were typically too small in terms of aircraft deployed and ordnance dropped to be effective. (ullstein bild via Getty Images)

With many of the units on Sicily transferred elsewhere, only three substantial bombing raids took place during November and December. On 23 December 1940 the staff of 2a Squadra Aerea was transferred to Padua for reassignment to the Balkans and reorganization with new units. Its previous units left behind in Sicily were reorganized under a new command, the *Comando Aeronautica della Sicilia*. The first stage of the Axis air assault on Malta was over.

Despite the Regia Aeronautica's initially optimistic assessment of its neutralization campaign over Malta, the actual results were far from impressive. By the end of December only seven RAF aircraft (two Hurricanes; one Swordfish; one Blenheim; one Maryland; two Wellingtons) had been destroyed on the ground by aerial bombardment or strafing attacks and only seven more (four Hurricanes; one Gladiator; one Swordfish; one Hudson) were lost in combat to Italian fighters. In achieving these mediocre results the 2a Squadra Aerea lost 12 C.200s and CR.42s, 21 SM.79s, one Z.1007 *bis*, and one Ju 87. From June to December 2a Squadra Aerea's bombers undertook a total of 403 bombardment sorties against aerial and naval targets on the island. Malta's airfields were never seriously damaged and neither were they ever put out of action. The dockyard at Valletta and adjoining naval facilities were still fully operational.

The failure to effectively subdue the island's aerial and naval facilities through bombardment was largely due to the Regia Aeronautica's insistence on bombing from higher altitudes. Bombs dropped from any aircraft at 15,000ft were subjected to strong winds and dispersed across a wide area around the intended target. It was estimated that when dropped from 15,000ft in ideal weather conditions during daylight hours, roughly half of the bombs dropped horizontally from a bomber using a manual vector bombsight would land within around 800ft of the intended target. Clouds, bad weather, and darkness would increase the circular error probability to over 1,300ft or more, far too broad for an accurate attack on an airfield, let alone any smaller targets. Furthermore the 100kg bombs primarily used by the Regia Aeronautica at this point in the war did not produce large enough blast craters to disable airfields, or larger explosions resulting in greater damage. During the Battle of Britain, Luftwaffe medium bombers attacked British airfields at similar altitudes, but effective damage was achieved through the use of larger 250kg and 500kg bombs, as well as through regular and sustained bombardment missions. A notable example was the Luftwaffe's raids against RAF Biggin Hill from 30 August to 5 September 1940. Eleven raids, made up of 132 bomber sorties, were flown against the airfield during that period, resulting in Biggin Hill suspending operations for roughly a week. 403 sorties over the course of six months with lightweight ordnance was simply not an intense enough bombardment campaign to maintain an effective state of aerial denial against the RAF on Malta – particularly if the RAF chose to contest this state and was in a position to deploy additional air units to the island.

And new air units did come to Malta. Due to the lack of substantial damage to its aerial and naval infrastructure, and the overall ineffective nature of Italian aerial bombardment on both land and sea, by mid-October the British Chiefs of Staff Committee decided that offensive aerial and naval units could be based on Malta and that it would be advantageous to do so, especially in light of the increased amount of Italian shipping crossing to North Africa without effective aerial and naval escort. On 28 October, the same day that Italy invaded Greece, Air Chief Marshal Sir Charles Portal, Chief of the Air Staff, ordered the transfer of 12 Wellingtons of No. 148 Squadron to Malta in order to begin a trial of bombardments against targets in Italy and North Africa. By the end of 1940 successful raids had been made on several cities on the Italian mainland and, on 7 December, a raid on the airfield at Castel Benito in Libya destroyed one CR.42, three SM.79s, and damaged an additional nine fighters and 12 bombers.

Perhaps the most devastating offensive flight from Malta at this time did not involve any bombs being dropped. On 10 November, a reconnaissance Maryland of 431 Flight flew over

The reconnaissance photo from a Malta-based Maryland of 431 Flight confirmed the presence of Italian battleships in Taranto harbour, and led to the famous carrier-borne Swordfish airstrike. (Print Collector/Getty Images)

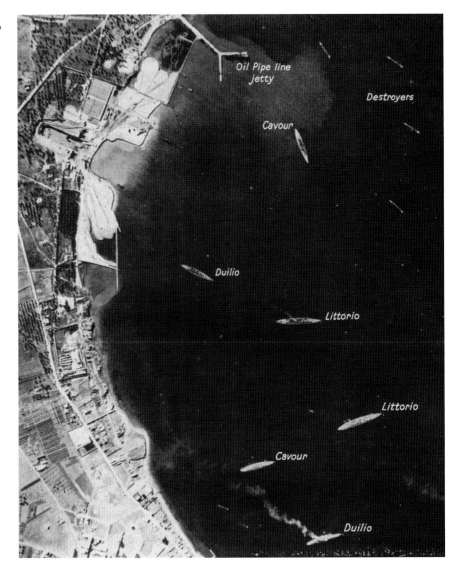

the Italian naval base of Taranto, confirming the presence of the Regia Marina's battle fleet at anchor. The subsequent carrier strike that evening by Swordfish from HMS *Illustrious*, the now-famous Raid on Taranto, disabled three Italian battleships, a move that compelled the Regia Marina to temporarily send the remainder of its battle fleet to Naples. While the raid on Taranto was not a knock-out blow to the Regia Marina, it appeared at the time to be enough of a setback to embolden the British to send air units and eventually ground units to mainland Greece. The shock suffered by the Italians over the Taranto raid was only made worse three days later, when the Greeks launched a successful counter-offensive on 14 November; by the beginning of December the Greeks had pushed into Albania. On 9 December the British launched Operation *Compass*, a counter-offensive in the Egyptian desert. By the time the British drive across the desert ended two months later, the Italians had been kicked out of Cyrenaica and the Regia Aeronautica's units in North Africa had been badly decimated, losing over 600 aircraft to all causes. Any remaining illusions of the war being a short and minimalistic affair were crushed by the weight of the disasters at Taranto, in Greece, and in North Africa. On 20 December Mussolini was forced to appeal to Hitler for assistance in the Balkans and Libya.

ATTACKERS' CAPABILITIES 1941–42
The Luftwaffe

At the time of Italy's entry into the war, Hitler had little interest in engaging his forces in the Mediterranean theatre, preferring to let Italy take the responsibility of tying down British resources there. The German high command only took an interest in the Mediterranean from June 1940 after the collapse of France, when *General der Artillerie* Alfred Jodl, Chief of the Operations Staff of the *Oberkommando der Wehrmacht* (OKW) or Armed Forces High Command, recommended to Hitler that an attack on Gibraltar via Spain should be planned; the closure of the western end of the Mediterranean would greatly disrupt communication and supply lines between Great Britain and its empire in Asia, and assist in compelling the British to agree to a negotiated peace. Both Göring and *Großadmiral* Erich Raeder of the Kriegsmarine were strongly in favour of the seizure of Gibraltar. Planning took place over the summer and autumn, with its conquest intended to take place in conjunction with the ongoing air assault against Great Britain. It was hoped to arrange Spanish entry in the war in order to more easily facilitate an attack on Gibraltar but Franco, aware of the Luftwaffe's failure to achieve decisive results over England by the autumn, insisted upon extensive promises that Hitler was unwilling to commit to. Despite these diplomatic setbacks Hitler issued *Weisung Nr. 18* (one of his *Weisungen für die Kriegführung* – Directives for the Conduct of War, or operational orders) on 12 November 1940, which outlined and formalized the military and diplomatic preparations for an attack on Gibraltar as Operation *Felix*. Part of *Weisung Nr. 18* included planning for a contingency invasion of northern Greece to counter British ground and air forces that were being dispatched to aid the Greeks against the Italians; German intervention in Greece depended upon the success of Italian operations. Hitler was less interested in supporting Mussolini's forces than he was in protecting Romania's oilfields, Germany's primary source of oil, from the British aircraft that were beginning to be stationed in Crete.

Generaloberst Erhard Milch addressing members of I./Sturzkampfgeschwader 1 in Trondheim, Norway in the spring of 1940, with one of the unit's Ju 87Rs in the background. Part of X Fliegerkorps, this unit arrived at Trapani in Sicily in late December 1940. (Bundesarchiv, Bild 1011-760-0165N-26, Photo: Lange)

General Francesco Pricolo speaking with Generalleutnant Hans Ferdinand Geisler, commander of the X Fliegerkorps. (Heinrich Hoffmann/Mondadori Portfolio via Getty Images)

Following the Greeks' pursuit of the Italians into Albania, however, Hitler issued a new directive, *Weisung Nr. 20*, scheduling a spring invasion of Greece. Air and ground units, some of which were earmarked for Operation *Felix*, were ordered to begin assembling in Bulgaria. Göring and Raeder fervently pushed for Operation *Felix* to go ahead, despite Hitler's intention to stabilize the Balkan Front to protect Germany's oil supply. Both clearly recognized and continued to point out the effect that the closure of the western Mediterranean would have on all British operations throughout the entire Mediterranean basin. A single concentrated campaign against Gibraltar, with or without Spanish approval, could avert the piecemeal distribution of German ground and aerial forces across the Mediterranean basin and close what was increasingly looking like a second major front of operations. This would stabilize the Italian situations in the Balkans and North Africa, allow them to regroup and deal with the remainder of British forces in the Mediterranean on their own, and most importantly allow German aerial and naval forces to focus their energies against the British Isles. Hitler disagreed however; the Italian collapse in North Africa combined with Franco's continued obduracy drove him to indefinitely postpone Operation *Felix* on 10 January 1941. It was a more efficient use of resources in his mind to stabilize the Italian forces in North Africa and eliminate any threat to Romania's oilfields – efficient in the sense that it did not take many units away from the primary planning objective on Hitler's mind, the invasion of the Soviet Union which was outlined in *Weisung Nr. 21* on 18 December 1940.

In *Weisung Nr. 18*, Hitler had already recommended the deployment of a small ground force and a Luftwaffe contingent to assist the Italians in North Africa. Commando Supremo, unwilling to share any Middle Eastern conquests with Germany, initially rejected the idea of German ground forces in North Africa, but was willing to accept German air support as the Regia Aeronautica was increasingly overstretched. With air cover for upcoming convoys of German units to North Africa badly needed, Hitler decided to send the Luftwaffe's X Fliegerkorps to Sicily beginning in early December to accomplish what the Italians seemed unable to do.

X Fliegerkorps

X Fliegerkorps had been established on 2 October 1939, after Raeder petitioned Hitler for the creation of a medium bomber unit which was trained for anti-shipping missions. Its commander, Generalleutnant Hans Ferdinand Geisler, had been an aviator in the *Kaiserliche Marine* during World War I and was well-versed in naval air operations. Throughout its first year of service the aircraft of X Fliegerkorps attacked merchant shipping and naval targets throughout the North Sea and in the English Channel. The selection of X Fliegerkorps came at the recommendation of Generalfeldmarschall Erhard Milch, who met with General Pricolo in Rome on 6 December 1940 to evaluate the most pressing aerial needs in the Mediterranean. X Fliegerkorps would be under the control of the *Oberkommando der Königlich Italienischen Luftwaffe/Oberbefehlshaber der Luftwaffe*, or Italuft/ObdL, a joint command that answered directly to the heads of the Luftwaffe and Regia Aeronautica and was coordinated by Generalleutnant Maximilian von Pohl, the Luftwaffe's attaché in Rome.

On 11 January 1941, Hitler outlined his priorities for X Fliegerkorps in *Weisung Nr. 22*, which included keeping the Sicilian Narrows closed to British shipping, preventing the Royal Navy from disrupting Axis troop movements and convoys to North Africa, attacking British naval and port facilities in Egypt and Cyrenaica, and supporting the ground operations of German and Italian forces in North Africa.

Aircraft

With such a broad operational mission, X Fliegerkorps was equipped with versatile aircraft that could undertake such a myriad of duties. The primary bomber X Fliegerkorps intended to deploy over Malta was the Junkers Ju 88 medium bomber. Junkers' response to a 1935 *Reichsluftfahrtministerium* (RLM) design competition, the Ju 88 was the Luftwaffe's first purpose-designed *Schnellbomber*, or fast bomber, and first flew in December 1936; the earlier Heinkel He 111 and Dornier Do 17 were both militarized conversions of civilian aircraft. The Ju 88A-4, the standard production medium bomber variant of the aircraft by 1940, would go on to become the Luftwaffe's most versatile aircraft, but over Malta it was intended to serve as a medium bomber. It had a smaller payload than the Luftwaffe's most numerous bomber at the time, the He 111, (3,100lb vs 4,400lb) but it had significantly better performance, being more manoeuvrable and having a maximum speed of 317mph, roughly the same speed as a Hawker Hurricane – a performance factor that occasionally allowed it to avoid being intercepted. Due to lessons learned in the Battle of Britain, by this time of the war Luftwaffe bombers were advised to conduct horizontal bombing runs at higher altitudes when flying over British targets with heavy anti-aircraft defences but the Ju 88 could perform the role of the dive-bomber when more accurate attacks were needed as the aircraft was equipped with dive brakes. While it had difficulty in near-vertical dives, the Ju 88 performed well in shallow dives up to 45 degrees and could deliver a much heavier payload than the Ju 87. The two Ju 88 Gruppen of X Fliegerkorps sent to Sicily in December 1940 were both from Lehrgeschwader I, an experimental unit made up of Gruppen of different types of aircraft that evaluated and refined combat tactics in different theatres. This was just the sort of tactical flexibility needed for a new theatre of operations.

LUFTWAFFE AIRCRAFT OF THE MALTA CAMPAIGN				
	Junkers Ju 88A-4	Junkers Ju 87R	Messerschmitt Bf 110D	Messerschmitt Bf 109E
Length	47ft 2¾in (14.4m)	36ft 1in (11m)	39ft 8½in (12.1m)	28ft 4in (8.6m)
Wingspan	65ft 7½in (20m)	45ft 3in (13.8m)	53ft 4¾in (16.2m)	32ft 4¼in (9.9m)
Powerplant	2× 1,400hp Junkers Jumo 211J inline	1× 1,184hp Junkers Jumo 211D inline	2× 1,085hp Daimler-Benz DB 601B-1 inline	1× 1,085hp Daimler-Benz DB 601A inline
Maximum speed	317mph (510 km/h)	242mph (390km/h)	349mph (560km/h)	354mph (570km/h)
Range	1,429 miles (2,430 km)	531 miles (855km) with drop tanks	1,305 miles (2,100km) with drop tanks	412 miles (663km)
Ceiling	26,900 ft (8,200 m)	26,903ft (8,200m)	32,811ft (10,000m)	36,091ft (11,000m)
Armament	5× 7.92 mm MG 81J machine guns	2× 7.92mm MG 17 machine guns, 1× 7.92 MG 15 machine gun	4× 7.92mm MG 17 machine guns, 1× 7.92mm MG 15 machine gun, 2× 20mm MG FF cannon	2× 7.92mm MG 17 machine guns, 2× 20mm MG FF cannon
Payload	3,100lb (1,400kg)	550lb (250kg) with drop tanks	-	-
Crew	4	2	2	1

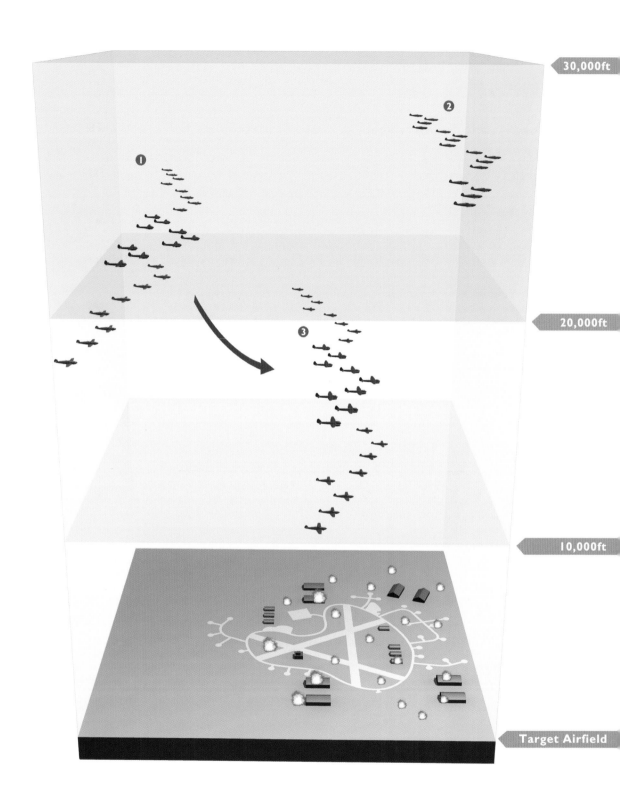

30,000ft

20,000ft

10,000ft

Target Airfield

OPPOSITE LUFTWAFFE DAYLIGHT BOMBING TACTICS

The Luftwaffe caused significantly higher damage to Malta's defensive infrastructure than the Regia Aeronautica in large part due to more capable aircraft and heavier ordnance. Junkers Ju 88s made the majority of Luftwaffe level bombing runs against Malta throughout 1941 and 1942. On a typical attack Ju 88s and their Bf 109 escorts approached the island at around 20,000ft **(1)** in order to force defending fighters to climb to a higher altitude. A Ju 88 attack group usually consisted of a three-bomber *Kampfgruppestabkette* leading two three-bomber *Ketten*, flying in *Staffelwinkel* (three groups of three bombers in V formation, flying in one greater V formation). Ahead of the bomber formation a group of Bf 109s would fly as a *Freie Jagd* (free hunt), or fighter sweep force usually at 26,000 to 30,000ft **(2)**, an altitude typically high enough to pounce upon climbing Hurricane and Spitfire defenders. The Bf 109s on the flanks of the bomber formation flew close escort at all times unless defending fighters made direct attacks on the formation. A further group of Bf 109s also flew above and behind the bombers and would break off to attack any incoming defenders. On their approach to the target Ju 88s and their close escorts descended to 13–15,000ft **(3)** and released their bombs from this altitude. Bombs were carried horizontally either internally or on external hardpoints on the Ju 88, preventing the wobble of vertically-dropped bombs from an SM.79 or Heinkel He 111.

The gyro-stabilized *Lotfernrohr 7* series of bombsights mounted in Ju 88s were more accurate at higher altitudes than the Jozza manual open-sight aiming device (however even under ideal bombing conditions the circular error probability of ordnance dropped from a Ju 88 averaged around half the bombs landing within 800ft of the intended target). While the majority of Luftwaffe ordnance was 50kg *Sprengbombe Cylindrisch* or thinly-cased high explosive bombs, it utilized more 250 and 500kg high-explosive bombs than the Regia Aeronautica. Furthermore the Luftwaffe employed 250 and 500kg *Sprengbombe dickwandig* or thick-cased bombs, ideal for use against the hard, rocky terrain of Malta's airfields or other hardened fortifications. The Luftwaffe also had the Junkers Ju 87 of its *Sturzkampfgeschwader* units for precision strikes against smaller targets such as anti-aircraft batteries, buildings, and ships. Ju 88s could also be tasked with limited dive bombing missions. This combination of better bomb sights, heavier ordnance, and access to dive bombers allowed the Luftwaffe to have more effective attacks on ground targets on Malta than the Regia Aeronautica.

The Ju 88 could also serve as a high-speed reconnaissance platform in its Ju 88D variant and a Staffel of 12 of these aircraft from Aufklärungsgruppe 121 was sent to provide strategic reconnaissance. In addition to its Ju 88s, X Fliegerkorps also had a Gruppe and Staffel of He 111s but they would see little action over Malta, being primarily reserved for anti-shipping missions and minelaying. Experience from the Battle of Britain showed that the slower and less manoeuvrable He 111s suffered a higher percentage of losses over target areas where fighter activity was to be expected. Strong fighter escort was needed and that was something that X Fliegerkorps did not have at the beginning of its Sicilian deployment, only possessing one Gruppe of Messerschmitt Bf 110 heavy fighters.

A Gruppe each of Junkers Ju 87 dive bombers from Sturzkampfgeschwader 1 and 2 as well as the staff flight from Sturzkampfgeschwader 3 were assigned to X Fliegerkorps as well. First flown in 1935, the Ju 87 had developed its fearsome reputation in the skies over Spain as well as the Luftwaffe's campaigns in Poland, Scandinavia, and Western Europe. Ju 87 units were badly bloodied in the Battle of Britain however; the aircraft did not fare well in a combat environment with heavy enemy fighter activity and anti-aircraft fire, proving particularly vulnerable in its straight dives and at low altitude when recovering from dives. But the Ju 87 was the only precision strike platform in the Luftwaffe's arsenal and was still very useful against targets protected by minimal anti-aircraft fire when properly covered by fighters. It was found to be particularly useful in the anti-shipping role, sinking numerous vessels during the Dunkirk evacuation and in the English Channel during the Battle of Britain. The Ju 87R was developed as a long-range variant of the standard Ju 87B production model, the main alteration being fuel lines through the wings to mounts for an external fuel tank under each wing. These gave the aircraft an additional 220 miles of range but limited its payload to a single 250kg bomb. The Ju 87s of X Fliegerkorps were primarily intended to be used for anti-shipping strikes but could be deployed against ground targets if needed.

X Fliegerkorps was provided with a better assortment of ordnance than what 2a Squadra Aerea had access to during its campaign over Malta and the central Mediterranean. Like the Regia Aeronautica, the majority of the Luftwaffe's pre-war bomb stocks were lighter SC 50kg and SC 250kg *Sprengbombe Cylindrich* general-purpose bombs. Throughout 1940 heavier bombs, such as the SC 500kg, SC 1,000kg, and SC 1,800kg bombs, were produced and X Fliegerkorps had limited access to them; they were primarily used as demolition weapons. Given the wide spread of bombs dropped from higher altitudes and the limited payload of its medium bombers, the Luftwaffe preferred to saturate general targets with more 50kg and 250kg bombs than a smaller number of heavier bombs. The Luftwaffe's 50kg and 250kg bombs were much more reliable than the Regia Aeronautica's equivalents. Furthermore the Luftwaffe could equip its bombs with its Type 17 *Langzeitzünder*, or 'long time delay', LZZ fuse, a delayed-action fuse that could remain active up to 96 hours after activation and which could detonate the bomb if moved. LZZ-equipped bombs required careful and time-consuming defusing by bomb disposal units, requiring the area around the unexploded bombs to be cordoned off and shut down until disposal teams could defuse and remove them. The Luftwaffe found during the Battle of Britain that LZZ-equipped bombs were particularly useful in aerial denial missions against RAF airfields; a single unexploded bomb near a runway could temporarily limit or suspend operations from the targeted airfield. Because of the already overtaxed condition of Italy's limited infrastructure and logistics networks and because the bulk of the Regia Aeronautica's transport units were tied down in the Balkans and North Africa, X Fliegerkorps would have to be responsible for its own supply needs. To this end the Junkers Ju 52 transports of *Kampfgruppe zur besonderen Verwendung 9* were assigned to Geisler's command. Because the bulk of X Fliegerkorps' supply needs had to be flown into Sicily from depots in Germany however, its operations were largely limited to its airlift capacity.

The only fighter unit assigned to X Fliegerkorps in December 1940 was III./Zerstörergeschwader 26, equipped with Messerschmitt Bf 110 heavy fighters. First flown in May 1936, the Bf 110 was intended to serve as a long-range escort fighter whose strength lay in its heavy armament (four machine guns and two 20mm cannon) and its high speed. In the early campaigns of the war the Bf 110 performed well against enemy bombers and in a ground support role, but during the Battle of Britain the type suffered badly in combat with single-engine Hurricanes and Spitfires due to its lack of manoeuvrability. As the Bf 110 had a longer range than its single-engine counterpart, the Messerschmitt Bf 109, the staff of X Fliegerkorps believed it could be successfully used for escort missions at sea. Most of the shipping between Italy and North Africa sailed on routes outside the range of the Hurricanes based on Malta, which meant that Bf 110s might only encounter RAF bombers, seaplanes, or carrier-borne Fleet Air Arm fighters which were much slower. III./ZG 26 possessed the Bf 110D version of the aircraft, a long-range variant which could mount a 900-litre drop tank under each wing. Bf 110s could also be used for ground support missions over Malta if needed, but single-engine fighter escort would have to be provided. Italuft/ObdL initially decided that the C.200s and CR.42s of 6°, 17°, and nucleo del 23° Gruppi C.T. would be sufficient for escort duties for X Fliegerkorps' missions over Malta.

While not initially deployed with X Fliegerkorps to Sicily, a small number of Messerschmitt Bf 109 fighters would later be assigned to the unit for air superiority purposes. The pride of the Jagdgeschwadern, the Bf 109 was the Luftwaffe's first mass-produced low-wing monoplane fighter, first flying in May 1935 and entering service in February 1937. The Bf 109 was very successful in the Luftwaffe's early campaigns but was occasionally bested in tight turning fights with less advanced but more manoeuvrable aircraft such as the Fokker

D.XXI, Morane-Saulnier M.S.406, and Hawker Hurricane. This tactical disadvantage became clear during the Battle of Britain when Bf 109 pilots clearly discovered that the Hurricane and Spitfire both had tighter turning circles. Bf 109 pilots learned to avoid turning fights with their RAF opponents and instead focused on dive-and-climb tactics, utilizing the Bf 109's superior rate of climb and friendlier stall characteristics; the fuel-injection equipped DB 601 engine allowed the aircraft to perform negative-g manoeuvres without the engine cutting out, unlike the carburettor-equipped Merlin engines in the Hurricane and Spitfire. The Bf 109 also possessed a slightly more-powerful armament of two 7.92mm MG 17 machine guns and two 20mm MG FF cannon. By the end of 1940, experience from the Battle of Britain had well acquainted Bf 109 pilots with the strengths and limitations of the Hurricane and Spitfire. With all Spitfires reserved for the use of RAF units stationed in the British Isles, the Bf 109 pilots that were eventually assigned to X Fliegerkorps exuded a great deal of confidence going into combat in a theatre where their opponents were exclusively Hurricanes.

ORDERS OF BATTLE: JANUARY 1941

REGIA AERONAUTICA
Comando Aeronautica della Sicilia (Palermo)
Generale di Divisione Aerea Renato Mazzucco
1° Stormo C.T. (Trapani) – Colonnello Alfredo Reglieri
6° Gruppo (Catania) – Maggiore Vezio Mezzetti (C.200)
17° Gruppo (Palermo) – Maggiore Bruno Brambilla (CR.42)
Nucleo del 23° Gruppo C.T. (Comiso) – Capitano Luigi Filippi (CR.42)
(note – 46 C.200s and CR.42s among the 6°, 17°, and Nucleo del 23° Gruppi)
30° Stormo B.T. (Palermo) – Colonnello Arnaldo Lubelli
87° Gruppo (Sciacca) – Tenente Colonnello Mario Giulani
90° Gruppo (Sciacca) – Tenente Colonnello Eugenio Cannarsa
(note – 14 SM.79s among the 87° and 90° Gruppi)
279a Squadriglia autonomo A.S. (Catania) – Capitano Orazio Bernardini (3 SM.79)

LUFTWAFFE
X Fliegerkorps (Taormina) – General Hans Ferdinand Geisler
III./Zerstörergeschwader 26 (Palermo) – Major Karl Kaschka (34 BF110D-1/D-3)
Stab/Sturzkampfgeschwader 3 (Trapani) – Oberstleutnant Georg Edert (9 Ju 87R-1)
I./ Sturzkampfgeschwader 1 (Trapani) – Major Paul-Werner Hozzel (35 Ju 87R-1)
II./Sturzkampfgeschwader 2 (Trapani) – Major Walter Enneccerus (36 Ju 87R-1)
2./Kampfgeschwader 4 (Comiso) (12 He 111H)
II./Kampfgeschwader 26 (Comiso) – Major Helmut Bertram (27 He 111H)
Stab/Lehrgeschwader 1 (Catania) – Oberst Friedrich Karl Knust (4 Ju 88A-4)
II./Lehrgeschwader 1 (Catania) – Major Gerhard Kollewe (38 Ju 88A-4)
III./Lehrgeschwader 1 (Catania) – Hauptman Bernhard Nietsch (38 Ju 88A-4)
1./Aufklärungsgruppe 121 (Catania) – Hauptman Arnold Klinkicht (12 Ju 88D-6)
Kampfgruppe zur besonderen Verwendung 9 (Catania) – Oberstleutnant Johannes Janzen (31 Ju 52)

ROYAL AIR FORCE
Air Officer Commanding, Malta – Air Commodore F.H.M. Maynard
No. 261 Sqn (Luqa and Takali) – Sqn Ldr A.J. Trumble (4 Gloster Sea Gladiator/16 Hawker Hurricane Mk I)
806 Naval Air Squadron (Hal Far) – Lt D. Vincent-Jones (6 Fairey Fulmar Mk I)
No. 148 Sqn (Luqa) – Wing Cdr F.F. Rainsford (16 Vickers Wellington Mk IC)
No. 830 Sqn (Hal Far) – Lt Cdr F.D. Howie (18 Fairey Swordfish Mk I)
No. 69 Sqn (Luqa) – Sqn Ldr E.W. Whiteley (4 Martin Model 167 Maryland)
No. 228 Sqn, detachment (Kalafrana) (4 Short Sunderland)

THE 1941–42 CAMPAIGNS
Battle for the Central Mediterranean

HMS *Illustrious* being attacked during the "*Illustrious* Blitz" of 10–23 January 1941, while the carrier was undergoing repairs in the Grand Harbour. (HMSO)

X Fliegerkorps' blitz: January–May 1941

The first actions undertaken by X Fliegerkorps in the Mediterranean were attacks at sea on 10 January 1941, against the Royal Navy's Force A operating out of Alexandria, centred around the aircraft carrier HMS *Illustrious* and battleships *Warspite* and *Valiant*, which was covering convoys coming and going from Malta during Operation *Excess*. Geisler instructed his crews to target *Illustrious* and 43 Ju 87s of StG 1 and StG 2, which had just arrived at Trapani that morning, were scrambled against her around noon. The Stuka pilots achieved six hits on *Illustrious* during that raid and two more hits were scored in afternoon raids by rearmed Ju 87s flying from Trapani and by three Ju 87s of 236a Squadriglia B.a.T. operating from Pantelleria. *Illustrious*, with her steering knocked out and flight deck and hangars badly damaged, managed to limp into Valletta that evening for emergency repairs at the dockyard. She was spotted there by an Italian reconnaissance flight on 13 January but there was little X Fliegerkorps could immediately do against this sitting duck of a target; the Germans had quickly used up all of their available ordnance during the raids of 10 January and subsequent attacks on British naval targets over the next two days. Geisler frantically arranged for the delivery of more bombs but they had to be flown in from Germany via the limited number of Ju 52 transports he had at his disposal.

Finally on 16 January Geisler launched a large raid against *Illustrious*, composed of 17 Ju 88s and 44 Ju 87s, escorted by a mix of Bf 110s, C.200s, and CR.42s. In the days before the attack Malta's anti-aircraft forces had coordinated a box barrage plan for the area around the dockyards in the hopes of disrupting enemy bombers as they made their bombing runs or dives. While only one of the attackers was shot down over Malta, the box barrage assisted in breaking up the attacks to the extent that *Illustrious* was only hit once that day. The Axis raiders were attacked by only four Hurricanes and three Fairey Fulmars (two-seat carrier fighters from *Illustrious*) but reports of fighter interference from his pilots compelled Geisler to change targets for his next raid.

On 18 January he sent 51 Ju 87s of StG 1 and StG 2 against Hal Far and Luqa airfields, hoping to disable them long enough for his bombers to launch another raid against *Illustrious* on the 19th. Luqa was out of action for a period but anti-aircraft fire and fighters from Hal Far disrupted the Axis raids on 19 January to the extent that *Illustrious* suffered no direct hits and sustained only minor damage from a few near misses. Once against X Fliegerkorps had burned through the majority of its ordnance in the raids of 16, 18 and 19 January, so aerial activity over Malta was minimal for the next few days. On 23 January *Illustrious*, sufficiently patched up, sailed for Alexandria. Once Geisler realized she had sailed he sent Ju 88s of 8/LG 1 to locate her but she was not to be found. The remainder of January was relatively quiet over Malta as X Fliegerkorps awaited further reinforcements, munitions, and supplies.

X Fliegerkorps' operational debut over Malta in January appeared impressive compared to previous Regia Aeronautica efforts but its overall combat results were disappointing. Its bombers failed to sink *Illustrious* despite significant resources spent to that effect. Geisler's bomber pilots had not previously encountered such a high concentration of anti-aircraft fire over a target before and this greatly affected the accuracy of these early raids. The number of British aircraft based on Malta which were destroyed in combat or on the ground from January 10 to the end of the month was not impressive: three Fulmars, three Hurricanes, one Wellington, and three Swordfish. Axis losses during the same period were much higher: nine Ju 88s, seven Ju 87s, one C.200, and two CR.42s were lost in combat while nine Ju 88s, one Ju 87, one He 111, and two Bf 110s were lost due to forced landings or accidents. In addition to these losses the Wellington bombers of No. 148 Squadron on Malta conducted several successful nighttime raids over the airfields at Catania, destroying an SM.79, a Ju 88, three Ca.133s, three Ju 52s, two He 111s, and two C.200s as well as damaging many more aircraft. The threat to Axis naval and aerial operations posed by Malta's

A strategic reconnaissance Bf 110 from 4./Aufklärungsgruppe O.b.d.L. flying over a Sicilian city, escorted by a C.200. With few bombers in Sicily during the first half of 1941, the activities of the Regia Aeronautica were confined to escort and fighter sweep missions over Malta. (Arthur Grimm/ullstein bild via Getty Images)

The '*Illustrious* Blitz', 16 January 1941

On the afternoon of 16 January General Geisler attempted to finish off the carrier HMS *Illustrious* which the aircraft of X Fliegerkorps had severely damaged at sea six days earlier. At around 14:00 17 Ju 88s and 44 Ju 87s, escorted by 10 C.200s, 10 CR.42s, and 20 Bf 110s, conducted a massed attack on the carrier which was undergoing repairs in the Royal Dockyard in the Grand Harbour. One by one, Ju 87s from I./Sturzkampfgeschwader 1 and II./Sturzkampfgeschwader 2 peeled out of formation and made their dives from 14,000ft against *Illustrious*. Miraculously only one bomb hit the carrier, causing minor damage, but the area around the dockyard was hard hit. Anticipating an eventual heavy enemy air attack after *Illustrious* limped into port on January 10, the antiaircraft batteries stationed around the Grand Harbour had coordinated a large box barrage to cover the area in the days leading up to the bombardment. Only one Ju 88 was shot down during the attack on the carrier but the intensity of the barrage made it difficult for the Ju 87 pilots to aim at and stay fixed in their dive path to the target, which resulted in the heavy damage to the surrounding area. In this scene, the aircraft of Major Walter Enneccerus, commander of II./Sturzkampfgeschwader 2, and another II./StG 2 Ju 87 dive on *Illustrious*.

Leutnant Erbo Graf von Kageneck, Staffelkapitän of 9/JG 27 and fighter ace, and his Bf 109E on a Sicilian airfield in the late spring of 1941. Kageneck personally shot down four Hurricanes during III./JG 27's brief tour of duty over Malta. (Bundesarchiv, Bild 101I-429-0622-29, Photo: Lempp)

aircraft was crystal clear to Geisler, who appealed for additional aircraft reinforcement, including single-engine fighters. By the end of January, thanks to reinforcements by convoy and transfers, Malta's fighter force had risen to 28 Hurricanes, four Gladiators, and three Fulmars, while 19 Wellingtons were also based on the island.

On 11 January 1941, Hitler issued *Weisung Nr. 21*, outlining the need to bolster Italian forces in North Africa in the wake of the success of Britain's Operation *Compass*. On 6 February, Operation *Sunflower* commenced with the dispatch of the 5. leichten Division to Tripoli. The 5. leichten Division was the first unit of what became the *Deutsches Afrikakorps* under the command of Generalleutnant Erwin Rommel. On 13 February the Bf 110s of 8./ZG 26 and the Ju 87s of I/St.G.1, and II/St.G.2 were transferred to Bir Dufan in Tripolitania where they were re-formed as *Fliegerführer Afrika*, still under the overall command of X Fliegerkorps but in a better location to assist the Afrikakorps. To supplement this transfer the Stukas of II./St.G.1 and III./St.G.1 were sent to Trapani on 22 February as well as the Ju 88s of III./KG 30 which were flown to Gerbini. Responding to Geisler's request for additional fighters, the Bf 109Es of 7./JG 26 and Bf 110 nightfighters of 1./NJG 3 were sent to Gela in February. Göring was reluctant to send additional reinforcements as Hitler had no desire to commit further resources to the Mediterranean with Operation *Barbarossa* on the horizon. However, Hitler's immediate attention was on preparations for Operation *Marita*, the invasion of Greece set for mid-to-late March 1941, and expected X Fliegerkorps to disrupt the British sea lanes between North Africa and

Greece. Malta was not specifically addressed in any of the above-mentioned *Weisungen*; at the time Hitler simply saw it as part of the overall operations of closing the Strait of Sicily to British interference.

After the '*Illustrious* Blitz' the Ju 88s and He 111s of X Fliegerkorps launched numerous small, 'nuisance' raids, typically composed of one to three bombers. These were largely conducted at night in order to minimize the risk of interception by enemy fighters and accurate anti-aircraft fire. Their targets were typically Hal Far, Luqa, and Kalafrana but on occasion they dropped magnetic mines off the Grand Harbour and Marsaxlokk Bay. As with earlier Regia Aeronautica raids, the minimal payloads dropped on these missions did not cause substantial or lasting damage to their targets. Accounting for his bomber losses during the *Illustrious* Blitz, Geisler was not willing to risk his bombers in large daylight raids without effective fighter cover to counter Malta's Hurricanes, something his Bf 110s and his ally's remaining CR.42s and C.200s seemed unable to provide.

The Bf 109s arrive

That situation changed on the late afternoon of 12 February when Bf 109s of 7/JG 26 flew their first mission over Malta, covering a raid by three Ju 88s. It was an immediate morale booster for the Germans as two Hurricanes were promptly shot down with no losses for the attackers. Most of the pilots of 7/JG 26 were veterans of the Battle of Britain, with *Jagdgeschwader 26 Schlageter* as a whole under the command of the ace Adolf Galland. 7/JG 26 itself was commanded by Oberleutnant Joachim Müncheberg, an ace himself with 23 kills by the time the unit arrived in Sicily. Although the Staffel had only 14 fighters, Müncheberg's experience and rigorous training of his pilots quickly assisted in shifting the balance of the campaign into the Luftwaffe's favour. Given some of its pilots' prior experience with Hurricanes during the Battle of Britain, 7/JG 26 tended to fly top cover for bombers at 20,000ft or above, knowing that the Hurricane's manoeuvrability and overall performance suffered at higher altitudes. The Bf 109s shot down another Hurricane on 16 February and another on the 25th. Toward the end of the month, after shifting units to North Africa, X Fliegerkorps received several new units in Sicily to replace those that were transferred and was finally ready to begin larger-scale attacks on Malta.

In the early afternoon of 26 February, Geisler sent out a raid composed of 38 Ju 87s, 12 Ju 88s, and ten He 111s, covered by the Bf 109s of 7/JG 26, 12 CR.42s of 156° Gruppo C.T., several C.200s of 6° Gruppo C.T., and Bf 110s of III/ZG 26; their target was Luqa. Eight Hurricanes of No. 126 Squadron scrambled to intercept the bombers but were quickly engaged by the larger number of Axis fighters. In the ensuing combat five Hurricanes were shot down for the loss of none of the attacking fighters; three Ju 87s and one Ju 88 were lost. With the Hurricanes kept busy by the fighters, most of Geisler's bombers were able to make uninterrupted bombing runs over the aerodrome, dropping more than 150 bombs. There was heavy damage to the runway, which was non-operational for 48 hours, hangars, and barracks, but the most significant damage was to the aircraft on the ground. Six Wellingtons were destroyed, and a further seven plus several Martin Maryland reconnaissance aircraft were badly damaged. Malta's aerial offensive power had more-or-less been neutralized in one successful raid.

After several days of relative quiet, Geisler launched another large raid, this time against Hal Far, on the late afternoon of 5 March. Around 60 Ju 87s and Ju 88s attacked the airfield, covered by Bf 109s of 7/JG 26 and supported by Bf 109s of I/JG 27 (temporarily in Sicily on their way to North Africa) and Bf 110s of Stab/St.G 1. Hal Far's runway was temporarily put out of action while the aerodrome's ground facilities were extensively damaged. A Gladiator and a Swordfish were destroyed on the ground while two Fulmars were damaged and two Hurricanes were lost to the Bf 109s; the attackers lost one Ju 88 and two Ju 87s. For the next several weeks the skies over Malta saw largely small-scale and nocturnal raids,

Oberleutnant Joachim Müncheberg, commander of 7/JG 26, meeting with General Erwin Rommel at an airstrip in North Africa. The Bf 109s of 7/JG 26 were instrumental in X Fliegerkorps' battle for air superiority over Malta in the spring of 1941. (Bundesarchiv, Bild 101I-432-0760-10, Photo: Opper)

as well as several fighter sweeps by 7/JG 26. Air superiority over Malta was gradually being achieved by the Axis and 22 March was to bring another impressive victory for Geisler's Bf 109s. While escorting a late afternoon raid by ten Ju 88s against the dockyard, 12 Bf 109s intercepted eight Hurricanes and in the ensuing dogfight managed to shoot down five without suffering any losses.

Taking advantage of the British fighter losses, Geisler launched three attacks against the Grand Harbour with his Ju 87s, escorted by 7/JG 26 and C.200s of 6° Gruppo C.T., over the next two days. Targeting the vessels of Convoy MW 6 from Alexandria, which had arrived on 23 March, the dive bombers achieved little success; their attacks were disrupted by the heavy anti-aircraft barrage around the harbour which had been steadily reinforced since June 1940, and three Ju 87s were shot down on the 23rd. One of the C.200s of 6° Gruppo C.T. shot down a Hurricane on 23 March and there were no losses for either side on the 24th.

Strategic considerations

Back in Berlin, the strategic importance of Malta in the rapidly expanding Mediterranean theatre of operations had become crystal-clear to Admiral Raeder, who had recommended an invasion of the island at a meeting with Hitler on 3 February. Raeder argued that the most effective way for the Axis to control the central Mediterranean was to occupy Malta and permanently eliminate the threat of British air attacks on Axis convoys to North Africa. He pointed to the failure of the Regia Aeronautica to neutralize the island's offensive capability in spite of six months of aerial bombardment and cited the Regia Marina's pleas for assistance against British aerial and naval attacks upon its convoys. Rommel, recognizing the threat to his seaborne supply lines to North Africa, likewise became a keen advocate for an invasion of Malta.

Despite the recommendations of these commanders, Hitler still insisted that the campaigns in the Mediterranean theatre could not detract from preparations for Operation *Barbarossa*. He did however appreciate his commanders' strategic appraisals and authorized planning for an invasion of Malta, to be undertaken once the course of the campaign in Russia had been decided. Recognizing the amphibious deficiencies of the Regia Marina, the German High Command decided that an invasion of the island would have to be an exclusively airborne German operation and over the course of February and March plans for this assault were drawn up. The aircraft of X Fliegerkorps would suppress Malta's aerial and anti-aircraft defences while the paratroopers of the 7. Flieger-Division would secure the island's airfields. Units of the 22. Luftlande-Division would then be landed on the airfields and assist the paratroopers in securing Malta's land garrison. To this end the units of the 7. Flieger-Division began immediate training for combat on rocky terrain. Towards the end of March however, following mounting RAF losses over Malta and the heavy raids on Hal Far and Luqa, Göring and senior Luftwaffe commanders began to reconsider an invasion of the island, believing that X Fliegerkorps was successfully neutralizing the offensive capabilities of the island, and wary of the extensive walls and fortifications on the island which would make rapid ground operations by paratroopers extremely difficult. Furthermore most Axis troop and supply convoys to North Africa were arriving unmolested, thanks in large part to the air cover provided by X Fliegerkorps. German strategists were falling for the same flawed analysis that their Italian counterparts had months before – that the lack of British offensive aerial and naval action from Malta meant that the island had been adequately subdued from the air.

Fallschirmjäger of the 7. Flieger-Division preparing for a mission in the Balkans in late April 1941. In the early spring the 7. Flieger-Division trained for an assault against Malta before being dispatched to the Balkans. (ullstein bild via Getty Images)

Ju 88 parked in front of a Regia Aeronautica SM.75 and SM.81 on a runway at Catania in the spring of 1941. Aircraft were rarely dispersed on Sicilian airfields due to the general state of Axis air superiority in the region – a situation occasionally taken advantage of by marauding British bombers. (Archivio centrale dello Stato 09912)

The successful coup d'état against the pro-Axis regent and government of Yugoslavia on 27 March 1941, two days after Yugoslavia's entry into the Axis Tripartite Pact, radically altered planning and operations against Malta. That same day Hitler abruptly ordered preparations for the invasion of Yugoslavia, and on 6 April German forces attacked into both Yugoslavia and Greece. This unexpected broadening of the Axis campaign in the Balkans required a rapid victory in order to free up German forces for Operation *Barbarossa*, resulting in the Balkan campaign taking precedence over all other ongoing operations. Luftwaffe units operating in the Balkans therefore received priority status with regards to fuel, ordnance, and replacement/reinforcement deliveries. As a result Geisler was forced to reduce the weight of his attacks on Malta, leaving X Fliegerkorps unable to carry on with the heavy raids it had performed in late February and in March. With Axis convoy protection still its foremost mission and with Rommel now on the offensive in North Africa, the limited supplies of fuel and ordnance allowed for only nuisance/nocturnal raids by X Fliegerkorps bombers throughout April in spite of having over 200 Luftwaffe aircraft now on Sicily. None of these raids resulted in any substantial damage. 7/JG 26's fighters, sometimes supported by Regia Aeronautica fighters, continued to escort bombers and reconnaissance flights as well as conduct fighter sweeps, but by the end of the month the situation for Malta's defenders had drastically improved.

Reinforcements for the RAF

Following the delivery of 12 Hurricanes during Operation *Excess* in January, No. 261 Squadron received only 11 more Hurricane reinforcements by early April. The increasing fighter losses to the Bf 109s of X Fliegerkorps compelled the RAF to organize substantial fighter reinforcements for Malta. The British aircraft carrier *Ark Royal* flew off 12 Hurricanes on 3 April and an additional 23 on 27 April. Also on the 27th, the surviving Wellingtons of No. 148 Squadron departed for Egypt and were replaced by the Bristol Blenheim IV light bombers of No. 21 Squadron. On 1 May, No. 252 Squadron and its

13 Bristol Beaufighter I heavy fighter/torpedo bombers were transferred to Malta as well. The Blenheim and Beaufighter were both well suited to anti-shipping missions and their arrival began to restore Malta's offensive aerial capability. Thus the tide over Malta began to turn as X Fliegerkorps was forced to scale back its operations, while the RAF began to rebuild its strength. The course of the campaign was decisively changed in late April when Hitler called off planning for an airborne invasion of Malta. A contingency operation within Operation *Marita* was an airborne operation to subdue the island of Crete and both the 7. Flieger-Division and 22. Luftlande-Division were training for this scenario simultaneously with the Malta scenario. With Yugoslavia overrun and mainland Greece about to fall to his forces, Hitler ordered preparation for the contingency invasion of Crete to begin on 25 April. To that end, 7. Flieger-Division and 22. Luftlande-Division were sent to Greece, ending any foreseeable German airborne operations against Malta.

The Royal Navy also took advantage of the German distraction in Yugoslavia and from 11 April stationed its 14th Destroyer Flotilla at Malta. On 16 April the flotilla destroyed the Axis' Tarigo Convoy off the North African coast; this success and the decrease of heavy German bombing raids emboldened the Royal Navy to station more vessels at Malta for convoy interdiction missions. Towards the end of April, Geisler responded by using his remaining offensive strength against the naval facilities around the Grand Harbour. His supply situation substantially improved following the rapid German victories in Yugoslavia and Greece at the end of the month. From 27 April to 3 May Geisler's bombers conducted several large evening raids, making high-altitude attacks over the Grand Harbour as well as dropping mines around its entrance. On 6 May X Fliegerkorps' bombers made a large nocturnal raid against Luqa and the Grand Harbour, followed by a series of substantial evening raids over the Grand Harbour and the airfields from 11–15 May. After the 15th Luftwaffe bomber activity was largely curtailed; most of X Fliegerkorps' bomber units were flown out of Sicily throughout May and were transferred to Greece for attacks on British shipping around Crete, prior to the island's invasion which commenced on 20 May.

7/JG 26's fighters saw extensive activity over Malta during this period, seemingly untroubled by the arrival of RAF fighter reinforcements. On 2 May, 7/JG 26 was greatly aided by the arrival of the Bf 109s of III/JG 27, temporarily posted to Sicily. From 27 April to 20 May these two fighter units shot down 14 Hurricanes and conducted a number of strafing attacks in addition to routine escort duties. III/JG 27 was transferred to Eastern

Hurricanes flying off HMS *Ark Royal* on 21 May 1941 during Operation *Splice*, one of the RAF's reinforcement missions to Malta. (Imperial War Museum A 4072)

SM.79s of 254a Squadriglia approaching Valletta from a high altitude. When the Regia Aeronautica resumed its smaller-scale bombardments over Malta in the summer of 1941, the RAF breathed a sigh of relief after the intense attacks of X Fliegerkorps. (Archivio centrale dello Stato 24389)

Europe on 20 May and 7/JG 26 to Greece on the 25th. As a stinging farewell, Müncheberg led a final eight-fighter strafing attack on the new airfield at Takali on the afternoon of 25 May, destroying four Hurricanes on the ground. 7/JG 26 had a particularly successful tour of duty over Malta, claiming 42 aerial victories, 19 of which belonged to Müncheberg alone; incredibly the unit suffered no losses in combat. By mid-June however the Luftwaffe was gone from Sicily, handing the responsibility for keeping Malta in check and for protecting the sea lanes to North Africa back to the Regia Aeronautica.

Malta had indeed been hit hard by X Fliegerkorps, especially compared to the Italian attacks of the previous year. X Fliegerkorps' bombers conducted 1,465 bombardment sorties against military targets on Malta between January and May, whereas 2a Squadra Aerea launched only 403 between June and December 1940. Unlike the Regia Aeronautica's small-formation raids with 100kg bombs, large German raids with 250kg, 500kg, and 1,000kg bombs heavily cratered the runways of the island's airfields and succeeded on occasion in putting them temporarily out of action. For a time both the offensive aerial and naval potential of the island may have been crippled, but it was never fully subdued by X Fliegerkorps. Despite the increased frequency of bombardment and the heavier weight of the attacks, this was still not enough of an effort to compel the British to give up on the aerial defence of Malta.

Indeed, the figure of 1,465 bombardment sorties is somewhat misleading as the vast majority of these were small-scale nocturnal nuisance raids of only one-to-ten aircraft. The heavy raids, while devastating, were not conducted with enough regularity to keep Malta's airfields suppressed. The craters on Malta's rocky airfields were easily repaired simply by bulldozing surrounding rocks and gravel into them, although this took time. Malta's ever-expanding anti-aircraft defences helped to disrupt attacks made against the naval facilities around the Grand Harbour and Marsaxlokk Bay. Credit needs to be given to the activities of 7/JG 26 and III/JG 27 which allowed X Fliegerkorps' bombers to operate with regularity, thus achieving an Axis air superiority over Malta for most of the winter and spring, but the RAF's fighters were never completely wiped out or driven from the island; air supremacy was unable to be achieved. Finally, X Fliegerkorps' limited supply situation as well as its many commitments in an expansive theatre of operations did not allow it to maintain regular, suppressive attacks and bombardments. As with the Italians earlier, Hitler's mistake not to identify Malta as a strategic goal and his preoccupation with other campaigns largely negated the bombardment efforts of X Fliegerkorps against the island.

Italy alone: June–December 1941

On 21 April Generalmajor Otto Hoffmann of Waldau, chief of the *Luftwaffen-Führungsstabes* or Luftwaffe operations staff, informed General Pricolo of the Luftwaffe's intention to remove the units of X Fliegerkorps from Sicily over the course of the next several weeks. Pricolo was also informed that the Regia Aeronautica would exclusively bear the responsibility of protecting North African convoys in the central Mediterranean sea lanes west of Cape Matapan in southwestern Greece. Pricolo protested this decision, claiming the Regia Aeronautica was incapable of performing this duty alone and in addition to resuming suppression attacks against Malta and keeping the central Mediterranean free from British naval interference. By January 1941 the Aeronautica della Sicilia had only 63 operational aircraft at its disposal, including 14 bombers and 46 fighters. The lack of bombers, a situation which remained throughout the spring, forced the Aeronautica della Sicilia to assume a defensive posture; but there were enough fighters available during this period to regularly assist with the escort of German bombers and reconnaissance aircraft, as well as conduct fighter sweep missions independently or in conjunction with X Fliegerkorps' fighters. The number of Regia Aeronautica aircraft in Sicily increased only slightly throughout February and March due to commitments in North Africa and Greece and also because Sicily's airfields and logistics networks could only support a certain number of aircraft at any one time. The stabilization of the North African and Balkan campaigns in late April allowed some reinforcements to be sent to Sicily beginning in May, as elements of X Fliegerkorps began to transfer, and by the end of June the Aeronautica della Sicilia had the following units on its roster:

7° Gruppo C.T. (Catania) Squadriglie	C.200
10° Gruppo C.T. (Trapani)	C.200
16° Gruppo C.T. (Gela)	C.200
70a Squadriglia (Trapani)	CR.42/Re.2000
30° Gruppo B.T. (Sciacca)	SM.79
31° Gruppo B.T. (Catania)	BR.20M
32° Gruppo B.T. (Chinisia) Squadriglie	SM. 79
87° Gruppo (Sciacca)	SM.79
90° Gruppo (Sciacca)	SM.79
99° Gruppo B.T. (Gerbini)	BR.20M
278a Squadriglia A.S. (Gerbini/Pantelleria)	SM.79
101° Gruppo B.a.T. (Trapani) Squadriglie	Ju 87R

This force looked more impressive on paper than it actually was; it constituted 161 operational aircraft, including 45 bombers, 16 dive bombers, and 96 fighters. This was a 25 per cent reduction in the number of combat aircraft in Sicily when the campaign

Generale di Divisione
Aerea Renato Mazzucco
served as commander of
the Aeronautica della
Sicilia from 23 December,
1940 to December 1941.
(collection of the author)

against Malta began in June 1940, and it was a 33 per cent reduction in force compared to Fliegerkorp X's numerical strength in May (101 bombers, 80 dive bombers, and 62 fighters). Furthermore it had much less offensive potential than X Fliegerkorp given its significantly lower number of bombers. Pricolo thus had good cause to plead with the Luftwaffe not to abandon Sicily, but in vain.

Generale di Divisione Aerea Renato Mazzucco, commander of the Aeronautica della Sicilia since its establishment, was given orders similar to those Geisler received earlier that year: neutralize British offensive potential on Malta as well as protect the Strait of Sicily and the convoy routes of the central Mediterranean. Mazzucco immediately realized that heavy bombardment attacks against Malta were simply out of the question due to the small number of bombers at his disposal. Between June and November his bomber squadrons would never have more than around 50 operational aircraft. Bomber reinforcements and replacements were unavailable due to the needs of other fronts (particularly North Africa where Italian ground forces suffered from a lack of adequate artillery) but primarily due to the aero manufacturers' inability to provide new aircraft and spare parts at a rate commensurate with combat losses and wartime wear-and-tear. This situation was exacerbated by the transfer of some existing and new-production SM.79s into *Aerosilurante* or aerial torpedo units beginning in late 1940. Additional dive bombers were unable to be obtained as the Regia Aeronautica was dependent upon the willingness of the Luftwaffe to transfer more of its own. The only type of aircraft which Mazzucco had in any respectable quantity was fighters and these were primarily C.200s. Mazzucco also had to deal with a significantly increased RAF presence on Malta as well as a greatly enhanced aerial defensive network.

The situation for the RAF on Malta immediately improved following the departure of X Fliegerkorps. From late May to late June Hurricane reinforcements and replacements arrived on Malta in four separate fly-off/delivery operations from Royal Navy aircraft carriers. By the beginning of July the RAF's No. 261 Squadron was reinforced by No. 185 Squadron, formed at Hal Far on 12 May, and No. 249 and No. 46 Squadron (renamed No. 126 Squadron on 30 June), both arriving via carrier in June. New bomber units and other reinforcements brought the RAF's strength on Malta at the beginning of July to the following:

No. 261 Squadron (Luqa)	Hurricane Mk I, II
No. 185 Squadron (Hal Far)	Hurricane Mk I, II
No. 249 Squadron (Takali)	Hurricane Mk II
No. 126 Squadron (Takali)	Hurricane Mk II
No. 800X Squadron	Fulmar Mk II
No. 252 Squadron (Luqa)	Beaufighter Mk I
No. 82 Squadron (Luqa)	Blenheim Mk IV
No. 148 Squadron (Luqa)	Wellington Mk I
No. 830 Squadron (Hal Far)	Swordfish
No. 69 Squadron (Luqa)	Maryland, Spitfire, Hurricane

Most of the Hurricanes on Malta by this time were newer Mk II variants, equipped with a 1,480hp Rolls-Royce Merlin XX engine which gave the fighter a higher top speed of 340mph over the 315mph of the Mk I. With this improved maximum speed and an increased armament of 12 .303 machine guns (Hurricane Mk IIB) or four 20mm Hispano Mk II cannons (Hurricane Mk IIC), the Hurricane Mk IIs were more than a match for the Regia Aeronautica's C.200s and completely outclassed its CR.42s. The Beaufighters and Blenheims were unleashed against Axis shipping and when not engaged with that were employed, along with the Wellingtons, in nocturnal raids against Italian airfields and other ground targets.

In addition to the increase in RAF aircraft on the island, Malta's anti-aircraft defences were substantially improved by the summer of 1941. Reinforced over the course of the previous year, the island boasted 26 heavy anti-aircraft sites mounting 16 QF 3-inch 20 cwt guns, 56 QF 3.7-inch guns, and 12 QF 4.5-inch guns by the beginning of July. This marked a 60 per cent increase in heavy anti-aircraft gun firepower from June 1940. By this time there were also around 100 light anti-aircraft guns. A report made by the anti-aircraft defence commander in early April claimed that heavy anti-aircraft batteries had accounted for 53 enemy aircraft shot down (confirmed and probables) from June 1940 through March 1941 and the light batteries had accounted for 11 shot down (confirmed and probables). The majority of the Axis losses occurred between January and March, a period that saw increased anti-aircraft gun deployment on the island, leading to the conclusion that the heavier barrage was achieving improved results.

The ground defensive measures of Malta's airfields were also greatly strengthened following the arrival of Air Commodore Hugh Pughe Lloyd, who was appointed commander of AHQ Malta on 1 June 1941. Lloyd initiated a massive construction programme aimed at creating enough dispersal areas with protected parking spots for all of the aircraft based on the island, which would be spread out and located far enough from the airfield runways. Thousands of civilian labourers were employed to dig and construct revetments and blast shields around these parking spots, and build graded taxiways from the dispersal areas to the airfield runways and maintenance facilities. At Takali caves were bored into a limestone bluff adjacent to the airfield, later to be used as underground hangars and repair facilities. Construction was

Hurricanes in the hangar aboard HMS *Argus*. In the absence of the Luftwaffe during the summer and autumn of 1941, the British were able to make a large number of successful aircraft deliveries via aircraft carrier to Malta. (Imperial War Museum A 18888)

This Hurricane Mk IIA, Z3055, was flown off HMS *Ark Royal* to Malta on 6 May 1941 and ditched into the sea on 4 July. It was recovered in 1993, restored, and is on display in the Malta Aviation Museum at Takali. (Stefan Stafrace via the Malta Aviation Museum)

also begun on underground bunkers to house the island's anti-aircraft, communications, fighter command, and radar control rooms. Lloyd also connected the airfields at Hal Far and Luqa via a taxiway and developed an auxiliary landing strip at Safi along the taxiway between the two airfields. Much of this work had to be performed by hand due to a lack of heavy construction equipment on the island and it was regularly interrupted by the need to repair bomb craters on the airfields from Italian nocturnal raids. Lloyd's airfield defence programme was not completed until the spring of 1942 due to the slow pace of the manual labour required, but it would prove vital to the RAF's survival later in the campaign.

Due to the strengthening of their RAF opponents on Malta, their broad operational mission, and their lack of reinforcement by any additional bomber units, the Aeronautica della Sicilia was limited to only a handful of offensive operational capabilities. The increased concentration of anti-aircraft fire and high number of RAF fighters precluded effective daylight bomber raids without a high degree of risk and Mazzucco wisely ruled against them. Mazzucco also realized that his units were unable to provide regular and effective aerial cover for convoys sailing to North Africa. Effective fighter cover was out of the question as the Aeronautica della Sicilia's C.200s only had an effective combat radius of roughly 100 miles from their airfields. A few experimental Re.2000s, equipped with additional fuel tanks, were assigned to the 70a Squadriglia at Trapani for convoy escort patrols but there were not enough of the aircraft available to make a difference. The Aeronautica della Sicilia's bombers had the endurance to remain over Axis vessels much longer than its fighters but without fighter protection they were easy kills for Hurricanes and Beaufighters from Malta. With large-scale daylight bombing and regular convoy escort both off the table, Mazzucco concentrated his offensive efforts largely on two types of attacks: nocturnal bombing of Malta's airfields prior to and during Axis convoy sailings and large-scale fighter missions, coinciding with Axis naval operations. The intended result was to maintain a degree of pressure against the RAF on Malta and disrupt the RAF's efforts to interdict Axis supply shipments. This would best utilize his limited number of bombers and his superior number of fighters, all while attempting to address all of the broad parameters of the Aeronautica della Sicilia's operational mission. Weather, limited supplies, and lack of effective naval coordination did not always allow these operations to be conducted when needed but it was a sound strategy given the limited resources at Mazzucco's disposal.

In an attempt to minimize losses to its bomber units, the Aeronautica della Sicilia conducted most of its bombardment raids over Malta at night. Most nocturnal missions over the course of the summer were undertaken by the BR.20Ms of 31° and 99° Gruppi B.T.; 116° Gruppo B.T. replaced 31° in early October and the BR.20Ms of 55° Gruppo B.T. were transferred to Sicily in early November. The CANT Z.1007 *bis* of 33° Gruppo B.T. replaced the SM.79s of 87° Gruppo B.T. on 29 August and the Z.1007 *bis* of 29° Gruppo B.T. were transferred to the Aeronautica della Sicilia on 2 September. The BR.20M units flew the majority of nocturnal raids over the island, the Z.1007 *bis* units typically being reserved for anti-shipping missions, but occasionally Z.1007s and SM.79s flew with the BR.20Ms. However, the number of operational bombers available to the Aeronautica della Sicilia never exceeded 55 during this period.

Bombers conducting nocturnal raids tended to attack from an altitude of 16,000ft. Small formations, typically two to four aircraft, were used for attacks against specific targets. 100kg and 250kg bombs were occasionally carried but 15kg and 50kg bombs were widely used, especially over airfields, as they could result in fragmentation across a broader area – ideal when trying to damage or set fire to parked aircraft. A preferred nocturnal tactic was deploying a small group of bombers, approaching singly and flying simultaneously over the coast at different points on the island, as it was believed that this dispersed the defensive response. Bombers on these multiple-point ingress raids typically carried payloads of 15kg and 50kg bombs to be released over a general target area. The following table illustrates the tempo of Regia Aeronautica's campaign against aerial and naval targets on Malta from June to November:

Members of 106° Gruppo B.T. playing volleyball in front of one of the group's *Z.1007 bis* bombers. (Archivio centrale dello Stato 04808)

MONTH (1941)	NUMBER OF BOMBARDMENT SORTIES	NUMBER OF FIGHTER SORTIES
June	73	311
July	127	296
August	45	211
September	61	125
October	59	154
November	150	159

In addition to the night raids, a handful of daylight raids were also launched over the course of these six months. Bomber losses of the Aeronautica della Sicilia were minimal between June and November with ten BR.20Ms, three Z.1007s, two SM.79s, and three Ju 87s shot down; a loss rate of only 3 per cent. The results of these bombardments were hardly effective, however, as only two British aircraft were recorded as being destroyed on the ground. Italian medium bombing tactics had not changed since the beginning of the war and conducting high-altitude bombing at night only reduced the accuracy of an already inaccurate method. The ongoing development of dispersal areas around airfields also reduced the effectiveness of the Italian bombardments.

Given the limitations of his bomber arm, Mazzucco attempted to use his fighter strength to his advantage, occasionally sending large numbers of fighters over Malta in the hope that his fighter pilots might be able to restore air superiority over the island through the attrition of RAF fighters. One particular method was to lure up defending fighters during Italian reconnaissance missions. A typical example occurred on 12 June when 18 Hurricanes intercepted an SM.79 on a reconnaissance flight, escorted by 30 C.200s of 7° and 17° Gruppi. Despite the large number of aircraft involved only one Hurricane and one C.200 were shot down. Another similar combat occurred on the mid-morning of 17 July when over 30 C.200s of 7° and 10° Gruppi, escorting a Z.1007 *bis* flying reconnaissance, encountered 19 Hurricanes over the island. One Hurricane was shot down for the loss of two C.200s of 10° Gruppo.

At the end of September Mazzucco ceased reconnaissance missions with a bomber and heavy fighter escort, due to the availability of camera-equipped C.200s and the arrival on Sicily in late July of the 173a Squadriglia aut. R.S.T., equipped with new twin-engine Fiat CR.25 reconnaissance aircraft. He could no longer afford to risk his limited number of medium bombers on such dangerous missions. Mazzucco also dispatched his fighters on several strafing missions against Malta's airfields during this period. In the early afternoon of 11 July the pilots of 10° and 16° Gruppi conducted a large strafing mission, with 11 C.200s attacking the aircraft on the ground at Luqa while covered by 42 C.200s staggered from 10,000–15,000ft. Twelve Hurricanes scrambled from Hal Far but in the ensuing dogfight neither side suffered any fighter losses; only one Wellington was destroyed. This was the only strafing attack during this period in which an enemy aircraft was destroyed on the ground. Overall the Aeronautica della Sicilia's fighter operations between June and November 1941 achieved little.

Fiat CR.25 strategic reconnaissance aircraft of the 173a Squadriglia aut. R.S.T. on Sicily. (Archivio centrale dello Stato 40185)

The Macchi C.202

By October it had become clear that the C.200 had become outclassed by Malta's Hurricane Mk IIs. In terms of performance it had been surpassed by the Hurricane's higher top speed and the Hurricane's substantially stronger armament made it easier for RAF pilots to shoot down C.200s, which still had the original armament of only two 12.7mm machine guns. This weak armament also was the primary reason for the aircraft's lack of success on strafing missions. By October around 20 C.200s had been lost in combat over Malta since June, while the defenders lost less than half that number of Hurricanes. But on 29 September the Aeronautica della Sicilia received its first Macchi C.202 fighters when the 9° Gruppo was transferred to Comiso, having recently been re-equipped with the new aircraft.

Macchi C.202 of 84a Squadriglia, 10° Gruppo C.T., at Gorizia during the winter of 1941–42. Several fighter units which had fought over Malta during the second half of 1941 returned to the mainland for the winter to re-equip with and train on the new C.202. (courtesy of Fulvio Chianese, Associazione Culturale 4° Stormo di Gorizia)

Beginning in January 1940, Macchi's designers had adapted a C.200 airframe to accommodate a Daimler-Benz DB 601A-1, the same inline engine that powered the Bf 109E. The C.202 prototype first flew on 10 August 1940. The new fighter maintained much of the manoeuvrability of the C.200 but the new engine gave it a maximum speed of 373mph. Two 7.7mm machine guns were added to the wings but it was calculated that additional armament would hamper the aircraft's manoeuvrability, the performance characteristic still prized most by Regia Aeronautica fighter pilots.

Getting the new fighter into service was a slow and laboured process however. A C.202 required 22,000 man-hours to complete, while it took Alfa Romeo over a year to put the DB 601A-1 into production as its licence-built RA.1000 R.C.41-I *Monsone* – and afterwards its factory was able to produce only 60 engines per month. Despite these setbacks, the Regia Aeronautica finally had a fighter that was clearly superior to the RAF's Hurricane and on a par with the Luftwaffe's Bf 109. The C.202 saw its first combat over Malta on 1 October when seven 9° Gruppo aircraft conducted a fighter sweep over the island. The C.202s were able to pounce on eight climbing Hurricanes and one of the defenders was shot down. From the arrival of 9° Gruppo in Sicily at the end of September to the end of November, the Aeronautica della Sicilia's C.202s shot down eight Hurricanes and one Fulmar in fighter sweeps and strafing missions over Malta for the loss of four of their own.

Despite the success of the new C.202s in their first weeks in Sicily, the Aeronautica della Sicilia had not surprisingly failed to achieve the mission objectives it had inherited from

Fiat BR.20Ms undertook most of the Regia Aeronautica's bombardment missions throughout the second half of 1941. (Archivio centrale dello Stato 44060)

X Fliegerkorps. Malta's offensive capabilities were far from neutralized; they were actually strengthened between June and November. As noted earlier the RAF suffered relatively low fighter losses during the second half of 1941 and the light and ineffective attacks on Malta's airfields allowed for a lengthy time of rebuilding and replacement. Hurricane reinforcements arrived in September and November via two carrier/fly-off missions. A number of Beaufighter, Blenheim, and Wellington bomber squadrons also returned to the island from the early summer onwards and operated for various lengths of time. By 1 December 1941, the RAF had 75 Hurricanes, 33 Wellingtons, 28 Blenheims, 11 Marylands, 25 Albacores and Swordfish, and a small number of Beaufighters compared to the 85 fighters, 40 bombers, three dive bombers, and six reconnaissance aircraft on the Aeronautica della Sicilia's rosters.

The anti-shipping operations of Malta's bombers over the summer and autumn took a heavy toll on Axis merchant shipping between Italy and North Africa. Malta's aircraft alone sank 132,689 tons of Axis vessels from the beginning of June until the end of October, out of 299,879 total tons lost in the central Mediterranean. Overall 23 per cent of the supplies destined for the Axis forces in North Africa were lost during this period with Malta's air and naval units claiming the majority of the losses. The RAF from Malta also took the fight to Sicily's airfields, conducting 59 bombing and strafing attacks from June to November which resulted in eight aircraft destroyed on the ground and many more damaged. By the beginning of December Malta's squadrons had wrestled air superiority over the central Mediterranean from the Regia Aeronautica and had blunted the Aeronautica della Sicilia's aerial neutralization efforts over the island to such an extent that surface warships and submarines were again regularly using Malta's naval facilities.

The Luftwaffe returns

In mid-September Admiral Raeder believed that the attacks from Malta on Axis convoys had become damaging enough to the Axis supply situation in North Africa as to warrant the return of X Fliegerkorps to Sicily, as well as more aircraft. Hitler initially disagreed, claiming that no aircraft could be spared from Germany's offensive in the Soviet Union, but by the end of October the increasing losses of Axis shipping to British air and naval units could no longer be ignored. After a period of negotiations and planning between Göring and Pricolo, Hitler ordered the transfer of Luftflotte 2, under the command of Generalfeldmarschall Albert Kesselring, from the Eastern Front to Sicily as part of *Weisung Nr. 38* on 2 December 1941. Luftflotte 2 was composed of II Fliegerkorps (under the command of former World War I ace Generalmajor Bruno Loerzer) and X Fliegerkorps, but most of the latter's units were stationed in Greece and the eastern Mediterranean. It was Loerzer's II Fliegerkorps, to be based in Sicily, that would be responsible for the central Mediterranean and Malta. Confident that victory over the Soviet Union would be achieved in the following year, Hitler also named Kesselring *Oberbefehlshaber Süd* (Commander in Chief South), signifying that Hitler now treated the Mediterranean as a formal theatre of German operations.

Kesselring had assisted with the development of the Luftwaffe since Hitler came to power in 1933 and for a time served as *Chef des Generalstabs der Luftwaffe*. He successfully served as commander of Luftflotte 1 during the Polish campaign and commanded Luftflotte 2 during the campaign in the West, the Battle of Britain, and during the first months of the invasion of the Soviet Union. *Weisung Nr. 38* outlined a similar

Generalfeldmarschall Albert Kesselring, commander of Luftflotte 2, speaking with Luftwaffe pilots in North Africa. (NARA)

mission for Kesselring as had been given to Geisler and X Fliegerkorps a year earlier: protect and secure Axis seaborne communications with Libya, support Axis ground forces in Libya, interdict Allied supply shipments to North Africa and Malta, and particularly, keep Malta under a state of *Niederhaltung*, or suppression – in other words a state of aerial denial.

To achieve the level of suppression needed to prevent the British from conducting offensive operations from Malta, Kesselring turned to tactics which his command had used during the Battle of Britain:

1. Light bombardment 'disruption' missions over the island's airfields would force up enemy fighters which would then be attrited by superior numbers of escort fighters. A disruption mission would consist of a small force of bombers, typically around four Ju 88s, escorted by anywhere from 10 to 30 Bf 109 fighters. Three to five of these missions would be flown per day. A small percentage of the bombers' ordnance would be equipped with LZZ delayed-action fuses. The intent was that the damage caused by the small bombardment as well as the time required to defuse the LZZ ordnance would disrupt or prevent operations from the target airfield until the next disruption raid occurred – thus imposing a rolling state of aerial denial.

2. Once air superiority or even air supremacy over the island was established, heavy bombardment attacks would be conducted against Malta's aerial and naval infrastructure.

3. Finally, Axis anti-shipping units operating from airfields in Greece, Sicily, North Africa, and Sardinia would interdict British convoys attempting to resupply and reinforce the island.

The key to the success of the first point was regularity; disruption missions would have to be maintained on a regular basis, and in strength, if aerial denial was to be imposed upon the RAF. It would take some time for Kesselring to build up enough ordnance and supplies for the heavy bombardments required to cripple Malta's infrastructure but towards the end of December he had enough units and resources in place to begin whittling down Malta's fighter strength. There would also be no shortage of German single-engine fighters for II Fliegerkorps' operations over Malta. By the end of December 1941 Kesselring had the full Jagdgeschwader 53 and an additional Gruppe of Messerschmitt Bf 109F-4 fighters in Sicily. The Bf 109F variant was a more aerodynamic version of the Bf 109E and mounted a more powerful 1,332hp Daimler-Benz DB 601E inline engine. To reduce weight the wing-mounted 20mm cannon of the Bf 109E were removed and a single 20mm cannon was mounted in the propeller hub. The loss of a cannon was lamented by some pilots but the more powerful engine and reduced weight gave the aircraft a maximum speed of 410mph and slightly more manoeuvrability than the Bf 109E.

Generale di Divisione Aerea Silvio Scaroni (centre, with sunglasses) assumed command of the Aeronautica della Sicilia in December 1941 and led the unit until January 1943. (Archivio centrale dello Stato 40714)

As the units of II Fliegerkorps arrived in Sicily throughout December, the Regia Aeronautica was undergoing leadership and organizational changes. On 14 November, Mussolini dismissed Pricolo as Chief of Staff of the Regia Aeronautica at the urging of Capo di Stato maggiore generale Ugo Cavallero, who had replaced Badoglio as Chief of Staff in December 1940. The Regia Aeronautica's failure to protect Axis convoys and to develop an adequate anti-shipping capability were cited as the primary reasons for Pricolo's dismissal but the air force chief had previously run afoul of Cavallero when he refused to allow control of the aviation industry to come under the office of Capo di Stato maggiore generale. Pricolo was replaced by Generale di squadra aerea Rino Corso Fougier, who had previously commanded the Regia Aeronautica's *Corpo Aereo Italiano* stationed in Belgium during the Blitz against England. The Corpo Aereo Italiano operated under the control of Luftflotte 2, and Fougier and Kesselring developed a good working relationship with each other – a key leadership aspect that would assist subsequent Axis air operations in Sicily.

Upon assuming command, Fougier took a realistic appraisal of the operational capabilities of the Regia Aeronautica, tempered against the immediate tactical needs of Italy's theatres of operations. The production of new fighters utilizing the DB 601A-1 engine, particularly the C.202, and putting them into immediate service was a paramount concern. He also recognized the mediocre capabilities of the Regia Aeronautica's bombers, particularly in an aerial neutralization role, and reduced the bomber arm from 16 Bombardamento Terrestre units to nine. Most SM.79 units were pulled out of service so that some could be transformed into *Aerosiluranti* units, due to the Regia Aeronautica's desperate need for greater anti-shipping capability; the crews of other SM.79 units were to be re-trained for service in fighter-bomber and night fighter units. Horizontal bombardment missions were to be largely left to Z.1007 *bis* and BR.20M units, the former predominantly focusing on daylight operations while the latter was tasked with nocturnal operations. Time was needed for more C.202s to come into service and for the bomber arm to be reorganized, and as a result the operations of the Aeronautica della Sicilia over Malta tapered off from December 1941 until March 1942. A further change initiated by Fougier in December was that command of the Aeronautica della Sicilia was given to Generale Silvio Scaroni, who with 26 kills was the second highest scoring Italian ace in World War I. As a former fighter pilot, Scaroni would bring useful experience and insights for the heavy fighter battles which would rage over Malta throughout 1942. However, by the end of December the Aeronautica della Sicilia had only a limited presence in Sicily, a number of units having been transferred to make room for the incoming II Fliegerkorps units.

ORDERS OF BATTLE: JANUARY 1942

REGIA AERONAUTICA
COMANDO AERONAUTICA DELLA SICILIA (PALERMO)
Generale di Divisione Aerea Silvio Scaroni
54° Stormo C.T. (Castelvetrano) – Colonnello Tarcisio Fagnani (C.200)
7° Gruppo C.T. (Pantelleria) – Maggiore Alberto Beneforti
16° Gruppo C.T. (Castelvetrano) – Maggiore Francesco Beccaria
377a Squadriglia aut. C.T. (Trapani) – Tenente Giuseppe David (Re.2000)
10° Stormo B.T. (Palermo) – Colonnello Ranieri Cupini (SM.79)
30° Gruppo B.T. (Palermo) – Maggiore Giuseppe Noziglia
32° Gruppo B.T. (Palermo) – Maggiore C. Alberto Capitani
173a Squadriglia aut. R.S.T. (Palermo) – Capitano Edoardo Agnello (CR.25)
278a Squadriglia aut. A.S. (Pantelleria) – Capitano Massimiliano Erasi

LUFTWAFFE
LUFTFLOTTE 2 (FRASCATI)
Generalfeldmarschall Albert Kesselring
II. Fliegerkorps (Taormina) – Generalmajor Bruno Loerzer
Stab/JG 53 (Comiso) – Oberstleutnant Günther Freiherr von Maltzahn (Bf 109 F-4)
I./JG 53 (Gela) – Major Herbert Kaminski (Bf 109F-4)
II./JG 53 (Comiso) – Hauptmann Walter Spies (Bf 109F-4)
III./JG 53 (Catania) – Hauptmann Wolf-Dietrich Wilcke (Bf 109F-4)
II./JG 3 (Bari) – Hauptmann Karl-Heinz Krahl (Bf 109 F-4)
III./ZG 26 (Trapani) – Hauptman Georg Christl (Bf 110D/E)
I./ NJG 2 (Catania) – Major Erich Jung (Ju 88C)
Stab/KG 54 (Catania) – Oberstleutnant Walter Marienfeld (Ju 88A-4)
I./KG 54 (Gerbini) – Hauptmann Georg Graf von Platen (Ju 88A-4)

Stab/KG 77 (Comiso) – Oberstleutnant Johann Raithel (Ju 88A-4)
II./KG 77 (Comiso) – Hauptmann Heinrich Paepcke (Ju 88A-4)
III./KG 77 (Comiso) – Hauptmann Egbert von Frankenberg und Proschlitz (Ju 88A-4)
Kampfgruppe 606 (Catania) – Oberstleutnant Joachim Hahn (Ju 88A-4)
Kampfgruppe 806 (Catania) – Major Richard Linke (Ju 88A-4)

ROYAL AIR FORCE
AIR HEADQUARTERS MALTA
AVM Hugh Lloyd
No. 126 Sqn (Takali) – Sqn Ldr Stanley Norris (Hurricane Mk II)
No. 185 Sqn (Hal Far) – Sqn Ldr James Pike (Hurricane Mk II)
No. 242 Sqn detachment (Hal Far/Luqa) – Sqn Ldr W.G. Wells (Hurricane Mk II)
No. 249 Sqn (Takali) – Sqn Ldr Hugh Beazley (Hurricane Mk II)
No. 605 Sqn detachment (Hal Far/Luqa) – Sqn Ldr Sydney Andrews (Hurricane Mk II)
1435 Flight (Malta Night Fighter Unit) – Sqn Ldr Anthony Lovell (Hurricane Mk II)
No. 18 Sqn detachment (Luqa) (Blenheim Mk IV)
No. 107 Sqn detachment (Luqa) (Blenheim Mk IV)
No. 40 Sqn detachment (Luqa) – Wing Cdr Laurence Stickley (Wellington Mk I)
No. 104 Sqn detachment (Luqa) (Wellington Mk II)
No. 828 Sqn (Hal Far) – Lt Gerald Haynes (Albacore)
No. 830 Sqn (Hal Far) – Lt Cdr Frank Hopkins (Swordfish)
No. 69 Sqn (Luqa) – Wing Cdr John Dowland (various reconnaissance aircraft)

The Axis' last push: January–June 1942

In late December 1941, as Rommel's forces were being forced back westward by the British offensive of Operation *Crusader*, the Luftwaffe returned to the skies over Malta for the first time in several months. Throughout the daylight hours of 19 December small groups of Ju 88s, escorted by a mix of Bf 109Fs, Bf 110s, and Ju 88C night fighters, attacked vessels of a recently arrived convoy in the Grand Harbour. During one of the raids the attackers were intercepted by 18 Hurricanes and in the ensuing dogfight a Hurricane was shot down for the loss of a Ju 88. On the next day a morning raid by four Ju 88s, escorted by 36 Bf 109Fs of JG 53 and C.202s of 73a Squadriglia, brought up 12 Hurricanes; one Hurricane collided with a Ju 88, with both being lost, and another Hurricane was shot down. For the defenders, having to fly up against a large escorting force came as an unpleasant development but it was one that was to become routine for the next several months. Naval facilities around Valletta and vessels in the Grand Harbour were among some of II Fliegerkorps' first targets as Kesselring intended to deter the Royal Navy from basing warships at the island. Malta's airfields were soon targeted as Kesselring's bombers began their disruption raids and the escorting Bf 109Fs began to take a toll on the defending Hurricanes. Ju 88s also began to experiment with diving attacks against parked aircraft around airfields and known anti-aircraft positions. II Fliegerkorps began averaging around four raids during daylight hours per day shortly after operations began.

On 26 December a force of over 30 Ju 88s and Bf 109Fs raided Luqa, destroying six aircraft on the ground and damaging several more; this was just one of six daytime incursions by Luftwaffe aircraft. Furthermore, although limited by the small number of bombers then at his disposal, General Scaroni resumed the nocturnal nuisance raids made by individual or small groups of Aeronautica della Sicilia bombers. After less than two weeks of operations, II Fliegerkorps had conducted 185 bombardment sorties and 476 fighter sorties by the end of the year, resulting in 13 Hurricanes destroyed in combat and another 16 RAF aircraft destroyed on the ground.

RAF reconnaissance photo of Castelvetrano airfield the day before the Blenheim and Wellington raids of 4 January 1942. Note the large number of transport aircraft. (Imperial War Museum C 4183)

Regaining air superiority

The successes of II Fliegerkorps in the last days of 1941 were particularly impressive given that Kesselring's force was nowhere near full strength. When operations over Malta began on December 19 there were only 26 Bf 109Fs, six Bf 110s, and 50 Ju 88s in Sicily. By 10 January 1942, II Fliegerkorps' strength in Sicily had risen to 79 Bf 109Fs (56 operational), 18 Bf 110s (six operational), 16 Ju 88C night fighters (nine operational), and 114 Ju 88A-4s (58 operational) for a total of 227 combat aircraft, 129 of which were operational. Further reinforcements over the next two months would gradually bring II Fliegerkorps' strength to a peak of over 400 combat aircraft. Over the course of the first four days of 1942 II Fliegerkorps conducted regular raids against Malta's airfields, resulting in the destruction of seven Wellingtons, one Blenheim, and one Hurricane on the ground as well as two Hurricanes in the air.

During the night of 4/5 January the RAF sent its remaining operational Blenheims and Wellingtons on four raids against the airfield at Castelvetrano; inclement weather over Sicily had forced many of II Fliegerkorps' and the Aeronautica della Sicilia's bomber and transport units to temporarily relocate to this airfield, resulting in a disproportionately large concentration of aircraft. Six Savoia-Marchetti SM.82 transports, four Z.1007 *bis*, one Ju 52, and one CR.42 were destroyed and another 42 aircraft were damaged. Precious aviation fuel, ground vehicles, and other supplies were also destroyed. As their force was highly dependent on supply by air, Kesselring and Loerzer decided that priority had to be given to immediately eliminating RAF bombers on Malta. After a week of bad weather across the central Mediterranean, regular Luftwaffe raids against the island's airfields resumed as weather permitted, with Hal Far and Luqa particularly targeted. By the end of January, 31 RAF aircraft had been destroyed on the ground and another eight in the air. A total of 1,741 Luftwaffe sorties were flown against Malta over the course of the month with only five aircraft lost to anti-aircraft fire and another seven to RAF fighters. Most losses were Ju 88s.

II Fliegerkorps continued its disruption raids throughout February and the first three weeks of March with regularity although Malta's defenders obtained relief on a number of days when bad weather kept the Axis attackers grounded. By the end of February a further 51 RAF aircraft, stationed on the island or simply in transit to other points in the Middle East, had been destroyed on the ground and another 22 in the air for the loss of 14 aircraft to anti-aircraft fire and 16 to RAF fighters. By early March the RAF on Malta had been reduced to 21 operational Hurricanes and its surviving bombers had largely been driven out. The Axis shipping losses in the Mediterranean had been reduced by 80 per cent from the autumn of the previous year and II Fliegerkorps had achieved air superiority over both Malta and the central Mediterranean. The reassertion of Axis aerial power in the central Mediterranean came at an opportune time as the Axis leadership began to reevaluate their strategic objectives in the Mediterranean theatre.

The question of invasion

In October 1941 General Cavallero and Comando Supremo had come to the conclusion that the invasion and occupation of Malta was essential for sustained Axis operations in North Africa and air supremacy in the central Mediterranean. On 14 October Cavallero initiated formal planning for an invasion of Malta under the codename *Operazione C3*. Both the Regia Aeronautica and Regia Marina were tasked with training paratroop and amphibious landing units for such an operation. By January 1942 Cavallero had convinced Mussolini of the necessity of the occupation of the island and then they approached Kesselring with the idea. While the invasion and occupation of Malta was not outlined in Luftflotte 2's strategic objectives, Kesselring immediately recognized the strategic benefits of occupying the island and believed such an operation fitted perfectly within Luftflotte 2's overall objectives in the Mediterranean. At the end of January Kesselring was beginning

OPPOSITE MALTA'S AERIAL DEFENCES: MAY 1942

preparations for a sustained bombardment campaign heavy enough to cripple Malta's aerial and naval infrastructure. It would take several weeks to build up enough ordnance and to make enough aircraft operational for such a campaign, for many of II Fliegerkorps' Ju 88s were damaged by anti-aircraft fire over the island, giving the maintenance crews a lengthy backlog of repairs to do. On 8 February, Kesselring met with Cavallero and Admiral Arturo Riccardi, who succeeded Cavagnari as Capo di Stato Maggiore della Marina in December 1940, and worked out the rough naval requirements for an invasion of Malta. Late June or early July was set as a tentative invasion period.

In February Hitler was petitioned regarding the Malta invasion plans by Kesselring, Raeder, and Mussolini. Rommel also agreed that the timing was right for an invasion of Malta and even offered to lead the assault himself. At the time Hitler felt that such an operation was unnecessary, citing the Axis' improved situation in the central Mediterranean achieved through II Fliegerkorps' efforts alone. He did allow contingency planning for an invasion to continue but the Oberkommando der Wehrmacht (OKW), unwilling to commit any ground troops to such an operation, clearly stated that such an invasion would have to be a largely Italian affair. In late February, prompted by Cavallero, an inter-Axis commission (including a Japanese naval mission on the request of the Regia Marina) was established to formulate the necessary requirements for a predominantly Italian invasion of Malta. Later in mid-April a formalized proposal would be presented to Hitler by Kesselring but in the meantime the Generalfeldmarschall was compelled to move forward with his planned heavy assaults on Malta's aerial and naval infrastructure; he had been informed by OKW that Luftflotte 2 would likely be sent back to the Eastern Front in the early summer to assist with the renewed offensive against the Soviets.

In February Kesseling's chief of staff, Oberst Paul Deichmann, had prepared an intensified bombardment plan, set to begin in mid-March, which was designed to meet the needs

Ju 88 crew playing cards and relaxing. II Fliegerkorps bombing missions were somewhat scaled back from mid-February to mid-March 1942 so that a large number of operational bombers could be built up for a heavy and sustained bombardment campaign later that spring. (Bundesarchiv, Bild 101I-359-2003-05, Photo: Röder)

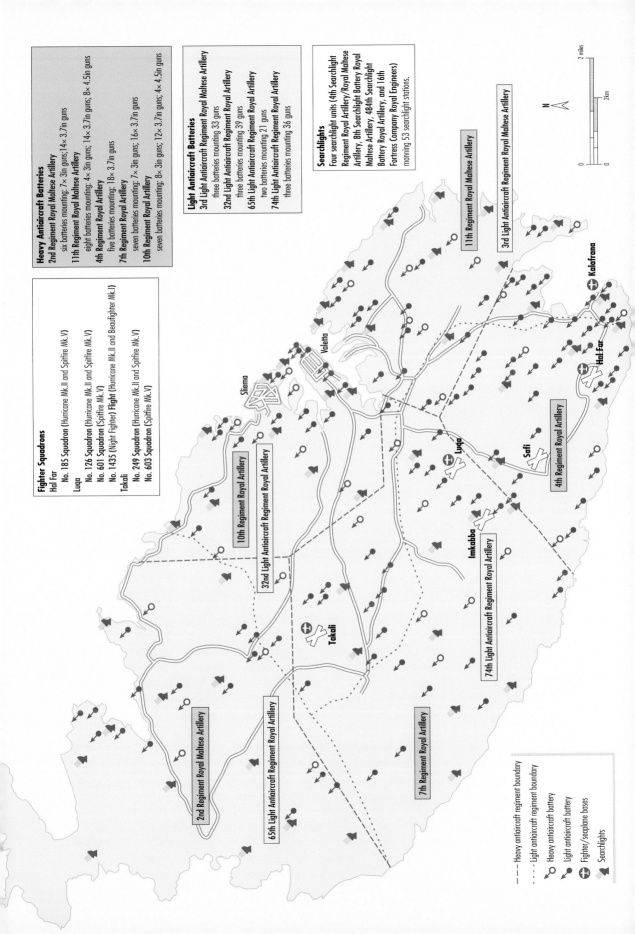

Heavy Antiaircraft Batteries

2nd Regiment Royal Maltese Artillery
six batteries mounting: 7× 3in guns;14× 3.7in guns

11th Regiment Royal Maltese Artillery
eight batteries mounting: 4× 3in guns; 14× 3.7in guns; 8× 4.5in guns

4th Regiment Royal Artillery
five batteries mounting: 18× 3.7in guns

7th Regiment Royal Artillery
seven batteries mounting: 7× 3in guns; 16× 3.7in guns

10th Regiment Royal Artillery
seven batteries mounting: 8× 3in guns; 12× 3.7in guns; 4× 4.5in guns

Fighter Squadrons

Hal Far
No. 185 Squadron (Hurricane Mk.II and Spitfire Mk.V)

Luqa
No. 126 Squadron (Hurricane Mk.II and Spitfire Mk.V)
No. 601 Squadron (Spitfire Mk.V)
No. 1435 (Night Fighter) Flight (Hurricane Mk.II and Beaufighter Mk.I)

Takali
No. 249 Squadron (Hurricane Mk.II and Spitfire Mk.V)
No. 603 Squadron (Spitfire Mk.V)

Light Antiaircraft Batteries

3rd Light Antiaircraft Regiment Royal Maltese Artillery
three batteries mounting 33 guns

32nd Light Antiaircraft Regiment Royal Maltese Artillery
three batteries mounting 39 guns

65th Light Antiaircraft Regiment Royal Artillery
two batteries mounting 21 guns

74th Light Antiaircraft Regiment Royal Artillery
three batteries mounting 36 guns

Searchlights

Four searchlight units (4th Searchlight Regiment Royal Artillery/Royal Maltese Artillery, 8th Searchlight Battery Royal Maltese Artillery, 484th Searchlight Battery Royal Artillery, and 16th Fortress Company Royal Engineers) manning 53 searchlight stations.

11th Regiment Royal Maltese Artillery

3rd Light Antiaircraft Regiment Royal Maltese Artillery

10th Regiment Royal Artillery

32nd Light Antiaircraft Regiment Royal Artillery

2nd Regiment Royal Maltese Artillery

65th Light Antiaircraft Regiment Royal Artillery

74th Light Antiaircraft Regiment Royal Artillery

4th Regiment Royal Artillery

7th Regiment Royal Artillery

Valetta
Sliema
Luqa
Safi
Imkabba
Takali
Kalafrana
Hal Far

- - - Heavy antiaircraft regiment boundary
· · · Light antiaircraft regiment boundary
Heavy antiaircraft battery
Light antiaircraft battery
Fighter/seaplane bases
Searchlights

N

0   2km
0   2 miles

of either a sustained aerial denial campaign or as adequate preparation for an airborne/amphibious invasion. As of 14 March 1942, II Fliegerkorps had 146 Bf 109Fs, 19 Bf 110s, 14 Ju 88C-4s, 131 Ju 88A-4s, and 25 Ju 87Ds in Sicily. Reconnaissance flights had shown that the RAF was operating its remaining fighters out of Takali so Deichmann calculated that a series of surprise raids over the course of an evening, when most of the RAF fighters would be unlikely to fly up, could put the airfield out of action until the following morning. At daybreak the next day a heavy raid, with LZZ-fused bombs making up a large percentage of the ordnance dropped, would ensure that the airfield remained out of action. With Takali's runways inoperable, the remaining aircraft there would be destroyed on the ground. Once Takali and its fighters were knocked out, heavy raids would be conducted against Luqa and Hal Far, and their surrounding maintenance facilities, until they too were rendered unserviceable. During the attacks on the airfields, some of II Fliegerkorps' bombers, particularly its Ju 87s, would be tasked with attacking anti-aircraft batteries in an effort to disrupt the increasingly effective barrages over the island. Finally once the RAF and its facilities had been neutralized, heavy raids would be conducted over the dockyard and other naval infrastructure until surface warships and submarines were no longer able to be based there. The date for the heavy raids to begin was 20 March. General Fougier, who had also been involved with the planning for *Operazione C3*, insisted that the Aeronautica della Sicila be involved in the neutralization of Malta's aerial and naval facilities, if for nothing else than for national prestige. On 18 March he ordered that fighter reinforcements be sent to Sicily, but they did not arrive until April and May as they were in the process of re-equipping with new C.202 and Reggiane Re.2001 fighters in mainland Italy.

The RAF on Malta had taken a particularly bad beating over the first three months of II Fliegerkorps' operations over the island. The large number of aircraft destroyed on the island during this period was due in part to there being a higher number of aircraft concentrated around the airfields than earlier in the war; during the period of minimal Regia Aeronautica attacks in the second half of 1941, the RAF felt increasingly at ease about sending aircraft through Malta on their way to destinations in the Middle East. The primary reason for the higher number of losses on the ground was that not enough blast pens had been constructed to accommodate all the aircraft operating from or transiting through the island. Air Vice Marshal Lloyd made the construction of the blast pens a priority and received assistance from the army garrison who tasked soldiers to work on the pens day and night.

Heavy losses on the ground would continue until more blast pens were constructed, but Malta's anti-aircraft defences had qualitatively improved since the German attacks of a year earlier. The island had received additional radar units in late 1941 and early 1942, including two gun-laying radar units which allowed for more accurate and concentrated barrages than the box barrages used earlier in the campaign. More anti-aircraft guns had been received from Britain and more batteries were situated around the airfields to deal with the increased threat. Malta also received a morale boost with the arrival of its first Spitfires on 7 March, 15 having flown off the old aircraft carrier HMS *Argus*. The situation on Malta had finally become dire enough (and Britain itself was now secure enough) for the RAF to warrant the release of Spitfires from Britain. The Spitfires sent to Malta were predominantly the Mk Vc trop variant which possessed a top speed of 362mph and an armament of four .303in machine guns and two 20mm cannon. A further nine Spitfires arrived on the island on 21 March.

Kesselring's blitz
As planned on 20 March, 63 Ju 88s, escorted by a mix of Bf 110s, Ju 88Cs, and Bf 109Fs, hit Takali in a series of raids lasting from dusk until the early morning of the next day with no RAF fighter opposition encountered. After sunrise on 21 March, 106 Ju 88s, escorted by around 100 Bf 109Fs returned and hit the airfield for two hours. A further raid of 70 Ju 88s accompanied by a heavy fighter escort hit Takali that afternoon just as Malta's second

Takali airfield under heavy bombardment by Luftwaffe Ju 88s on 1 April 1942. (ullstein bild via Getty Images)

batch of Spitfires arrived over the island. Takali was put out of action by these raids but the runway was made operable on the evening of 22 March to allow the surviving Spitfires and Hurricanes to fly to the other airfields. Two Spitfires, four Hurricanes, one Beaufighter, one Maryland, and one Wellington were destroyed and a further 26 aircraft were damaged. For the next several days Kesselring deviated from his plan against the airfields to focus on sinking ships of a convoy that reached the Grand Harbour on 23 March. Smaller raids over the airfields took place for the remainder of the month. The tally for the month was 95 RAF aircraft destroyed on the ground and 34 in the air. II Fliegerkorps had conducted 859 daylight and 350 nocturnal bombardment sorties against Malta over the course of March. Despite reinforcements of ten Hurricanes from North Africa on 27 March and an additional nine Spitfires on 29 March the RAF was down to only a handful of operational fighters on the island at the beginning of April.

Intercept of Operation *Bowery*: 9 May 1942

In this scene a flight of CANT Z.1007 *bis* bombers from 50° Gruppo B.T., having hit Takali airfield, come under attack from Spitfire Mk Vs of No. 126 Squadron as the bombers head away from Malta towards the northwest at around 17:55. Several Macchi C.202 escorts swing around from the south to engage the Spitfires.

On 9 May 1942, Kesselring launched the last major air assaults of his spring aerial denial campaign against Malta. Italian intelligence had learned of an upcoming Spitfire reinforcement (Operation *Bowery*) to the island and Kesselring hoped to destroy the new arrivals on the ground after they had landed. Large numbers of Bf 109s and C.202s, in some cases up to 40, escorted groups of Ju 88s, Ju 87s, and Z.1007 *bis* on seven bombardment raids throughout the day. If the Spitfires were not destroyed on the ground, they could then be engaged by the large number of Axis fighter escorts. The RAF on Malta made a concentrated effort to keep as many of its fighters, including the newly arrived Spitfires, in the air as possible in order to avoid being caught defenceless on the ground. This involved immediately refuelling aircraft upon landing and rotating pilots throughout the day in order to ensure that there was a near-constant RAF fighter presence over the island. In spite of the large Axis commitment and the many dogfights over the island on 9 May, only four Spitfires were shot down for the loss of a single Bf 109. Elements of II Fliegerkorps began transferring out of Sicily shortly thereafter and the Axis was never again able to win air superiority over the island.

Ju 87 taking off from an airfield in early 1942. (Past Pix/SSPL/Getty Images)

On 2 April Kesselring's bombers returned in force and for the remainder of the month his units were able to launch an average of two heavy raids per day, typically consisting of 30 to 70 bombers and dive bombers with a heavy fighter escort. The airfields, the dockyard and naval facilities around the Grand Harbour, and the submarine base on Manoel Island were the regular targets. Interception by RAF fighters became infrequent due to the losses inflicted on the defenders; on some days the RAF could not put a single fighter up. Ju 88s made shallow dive attacks for greater accuracy, but were compelled to stay above 6,000ft due to the heavy concentration of light anti-aircraft guns around the airfields and Grand Harbour. Horizontal bombing attacks from 13,000ft and above were deemed safer. Ju 87s were frequently employed in attacks on anti-aircraft batteries over the course of the month in an attempt to alleviate the pressure on the Ju 88s. Few anti-aircraft guns were destroyed, however, and the terror effect of the dive-bombing attacks rarely disrupted anti-aircraft fire as II Fliegerkorps' strategists assumed.

Given the reduced presence of enemy fighters a number of Bf 109Fs were occasionally employed in the *Jagdbomber* (fighter bomber) or *Jabo* role, carrying a single 250kg bomb under the fuselage. In the latter part of the month the Aeronautica della Sicilia began limited daylight operations over Malta but its bombardment sorties paled in comparison to those of II Fliegerkorps. Regia Aeronautica nocturnal bombardment raids were increased but it was the arrival of Italian fighter reinforcements that aided II Fliegerkorps' efforts. 9° and 10° Gruppi C.T. arrived in Sicily on 15 April with new C.202 fighters and 2° Gruppo C.T., with its Re.2001s, arrived on 4 May. As for the RAF, seven Hurricanes arrived from North Africa on 19 April but a substantial reinforcement of 46 Spitfires, flown off HMS *Eagle* and USS *Wasp* in a joint Allied operation, arrived on 21 April. These reinforcements made little difference as over the course of April, 20 Spitfires and 11 Hurricanes had been shot down and a further 22 Spitfires and 19 Hurricanes were destroyed on the ground. Only seven Spitfires remained operational by 1 May. II Fliegerkorps had conducted an oppressive

4,338 bombardment sorties and 4,132 fighter sorties over Malta in April alone. A total of 2,395 tons of bombs were dropped on Malta's airfields while the naval facilities around the Grand Harbour received 3,156 tons of bombs.

While II Fliegerkorps had lost 55 bombers and 68 fighters to enemy fighters and anti-aircraft fire for the months of March and April, between his remaining forces and those of the Aeronautica della Sicilia Kesselring had enough strength to maintain the aerial neutralization of Malta. The heavy bombardment raids continued into the first week of May, with the Aeronautica della Sicilia adding Z.1007 *bis* and C.202s to II Fliegerkorps' attacks. 9 May saw a high degree of aerial activity over the island as 60 Spitfires arrived on the island throughout the morning, having flown off from HMS *Eagle* and USS *Wasp* in the western Mediterranean. Geisler and Scaroni launched eight bombardment raids over the course of the day in an effort to destroy as many of the newly arrived fighters as possible but losses to both sides were minimal: only two Spitfires and one Bf 109F were destroyed.

On the following day the Axis forces suffered disproportionate losses to the newly arrived Spitfires; over the course of four raids four Ju 87s, four Ju 88s, three Bf 109Fs, one Z.1007 *bis*, and one C.202 were lost for only three Spitfires shot down. Expecting heavy retaliatory raids on 11 May, the RAF on Malta prepared for another aerial onslaught. The raids came but they were much lighter than those of the previous weeks, and the raids remained lighter for the remainder of the month. What was more encouraging to the RAF pilots was that they were encountering an increasing number of Regia Aeronautica aircraft over the island. Intelligence and reconnaissance confirmed suspicions: the Luftwaffe units were departing Sicily and the Regia Aeronautica was increasingly assuming control of the campaign over Malta. May saw only 342 daylight bombardment sorties over the island with 232 nocturnal bombardment sorties. For the month of June there were only 24 daylight bombardment sorties and 364 nocturnal sorties. To the RAF it appeared as if the tide had turned and Malta's fighter pilots had blunted the Axis aerial offensive.

Redeployment

The tide of the campaign was to turn in favour of the British but not because Malta's Spitfires had achieved victory in the air. Quite the contrary actually; by 10 May Kesselring believed that his force's efforts had successfully neutralized the aerial and naval offensive capabilities of Malta and declared Axis aerial supremacy over the island and central Mediterranean. During the first five months of 1942 only 7 per cent of Axis shipping to North Africa was lost and Rommel was allowed to rebuild his forces. Most RAF bomber units had been driven from the island as well as the surface warships and submarines from its naval bases. While never completely destroyed or rendered inoperative for lengthy periods of time, Malta's airfields and naval facilities were heavily damaged, making operations from them difficult. Shortages in supplies caused by the aerial interdiction of supply vessels also limited the island's military operations. Furthermore II Fliegerkorps had demonstrated that it was able to cripple Malta's fighter force despite the arrival of a sizeable number of Spitfires throughout March and April; the RAF had again been brought nearly to its knees when the next batch of Spitfires arrived on 9 May. Kesselring had more than accomplished Luftflotte 2's original mission and had severely weakened the RAF in anticipation of an Axis invasion of the island. The tide in the campaign began to turn in May and June because most of the units of Luftflotte 2 departed Sicily for service in other areas. By mid-June the Luftwaffe's presence in Sicily consisted only of the 27 Bf 109Fs of Stab/JG 53 and II/JG 53, the 21 Ju 88s of KGr 606 and KGr 806, and the reconnaissance aircraft of 1/Aufkl.Gr. 121. Kesselring's forces had not been beaten; they had simply been transferred.

In early April Kesselring and Cavallero worked out a version of *Operazione C3* in which the majority of forces committed would be Italian; the primary units needed from the Germans were paratroop divisions, transport aircraft, and Luftwaffe fighters and bombers.

Bf 109G and Bf 109Fs of Jagdgeschwader 53 in Sicily. (Bundesarchiv, Bild 101I-468-1404-28, Photo: Ketelhohn, Karl)

Mussolini approved the plan and it was presented to Hitler on 18 April. In the light of Kesselring winning Axis air superiority over Malta and the central Mediterranean, Hitler agreed to the invasion and ordered German planning for the operation to begin under the codename Operation *Herkules* on 21 April. Generalleutnant Kurt Student and his XI. Fliegerkorps were dispatched to Italy to begin training for the operation. Comando Supremo calculated that the Italian forces committed to *Operazione C3* would be ready to begin the invasion sometime in July. At the same time across the Mediterranean Rommel was planning a large operation of his own, Operation *Venezia*, an offensive aimed at capturing Tobruk and pushing the British back across the Egyptian border. As Rommel would be ready for his offensive before the Italians were ready for *Operazione C3*, and because units of Luftflotte 2 would be needed for both operations, Hitler decided on 30 April that Rommel's offensive would take place before the invasion of Malta.

Units from Luftflotte 2 would be sent to North Africa to assist with Operation *Venezia* and once Rommel reached the Egyptian frontier, he would cease his attack and Luftwaffe units would be transferred back to Sicily for operations against Malta. Mussolini agreed with Hitler's assessment as it allowed his armed forces the time they needed to prepare for the invasion. In mid-May Kesselring diverted some of Luftflotte 2's units to North Africa and Göring ordered others to the Eastern Front for the German summer offensive against the Soviet Union. At the time Kesselring reasoned that his remaining forces and those of the Aeronautica della Sicilia could continue the previous disruption mission over the island to keep the RAF in check until Luftwaffe units could be transferred back to Sicily from North Africa.

Suddenly in mid-June Hitler recalled General Student to Berlin and ordered him not to return to Italy. On 15 June Hitler refused a request from the Regia Marina for the fuel required for *Operazione C3*. Hitler was having second thoughts about the invasion of Malta, doubting the ability of the Italian armed forces to pull off such a complex operation, and wary of having his airborne forces, carefully rebuilt after suffering crippling casualties in Crete the previous year, squandered in an operation he felt was unlikely to succeed.

Meanwhile Rommel, who had launched his offensive on 26 May, captured Tobruk on 21 June and requested permission to exploit his victory and pursue the British into Egypt. Rommel needed immediate supplies and reinforcements, some of which would have to come from those reserved for Malta. That evening Hitler decided to suspend Operation *Herkules* and gave Rommel the green light to proceed into Egypt, despite the risk of allowing Malta to once again become a threat to Rommel's seaborne supply lines in his rear. The OKW concurred, unwilling to siphon units and supplies away from the Eastern Front. Kesselring and Cavallero, shocked by Hitler's about-face, met with General Fougier and other Italian commanders on 25 June to determine if *Operazione C3* could be carried out by Italian forces alone. Fougier stated that the Aeronautica della Sicilia could not be supplied with enough bombers to carry out the heavy daylight bombardments that II Fliegerkorps had, and that his bombers were ill-equipped to conduct daylight operations against Malta's aerial defences without additional Luftwaffe support. Cavallero quickly concluded that without German supplies, particularly oil, *Operazione C3* could not move forward.

By the end of June 1942 all serious Axis planning for an invasion of Malta abruptly ceased. The shelving of the *Operazione C3/Unternehem Herkules* plans brought an effective end to the Axis campaign of aerial denial over Malta. The RAF took advantage of the decreased aerial activity in June and heavily reinforced the island with Spitfires; soon fighter-bombers and bombers returned to Malta's airfields to resume attacks on Axis convoys. Heavy fighting continued in the skies over Malta through the end of October but the focus for the Axis was no longer the neutralization of Malta's aerial and naval infrastructure; rather, it was the protection of Rommel's supply lines and parrying RAF and Royal Navy attempts to sever them. By the end of November 1942, Rommel's defeat at the battle of El Alamein and the Allied landings in Morocco and Algeria forced the Luftwaffe and Regia Aeronautica to send most of their remaining forces in Sicily to North Africa.

The war in North Africa turned in late 1942, forcing the redeployment of most of the Luftwaffe's Sicily-based units to assist. Six months later the North Africa campaign had been lost and Sicily itself was shortly to be invaded. (ullstein bild via Getty Images)

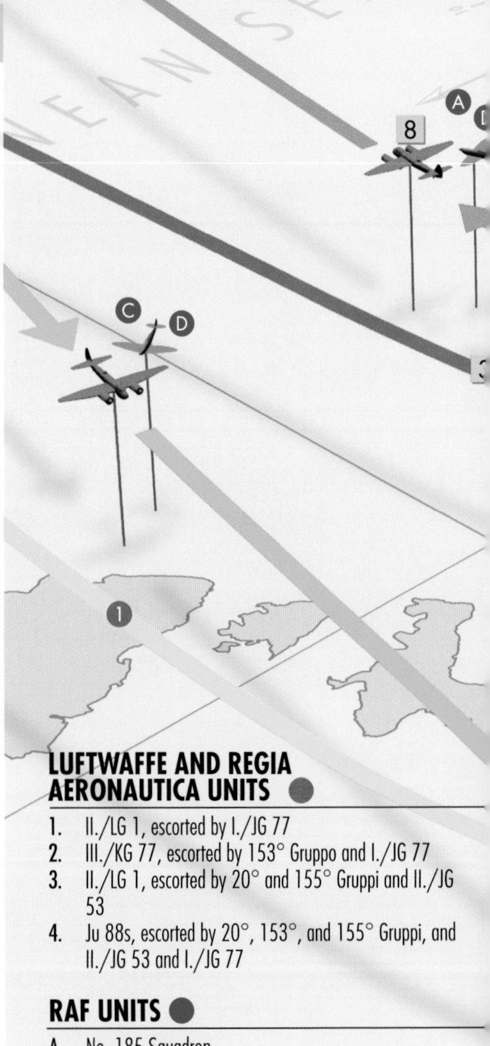

FIRST AND SECOND RAIDS

1. 0630–0700hrs: seven Ju 88s and 35 Bf 109s head for Malta for a raid on Luqa airfield. At 0635hrs, Spitfires begin to be scrambled from Hal Far, Luqa, and Takali. Eight Spitfires of No. 185 Sqn (Hal Far) are attacked shortly before 0700hrs by Bf 109s and held at bay north of the island.

2. 0705–0720hrs: Ju 88s descend and attack Luqa. Eight Spitfires of No. 249 Sqn (Takali) intercept just north of Malta and a Ju 88 is shot down. A Bf 109 damages a No. 249 Sqn Spitfire; it crash-lands at Takali.

3. 0720–0730hrs: eight Spitfires of No. 1435 Sqn (Luqa) and two from No. 185 Sqn pursue as the attackers turn back for Sicily and briefly parry with JG 77's fighters.

4. 0930–0945hrs: six Ju 88s, 28 C.202s and 36 Bf 109s approach for another raid on Luqa. Sixteen Spitfires of No. 126 (Luqa) and No. 1435 Sqn are scrambled at 0935hrs and are quickly engaged.

5. 0945–1000hrs: a Ju 88 is shot down north of Gozo but the rest bomb Luqa and Safi. The attackers turn to the north and withdraw without further loss.

THIRD AND FOURTH RAIDS

6. 1235–1315hrs: six Ju 88s, 25 C.202s, and 40 Bf 109s approach. Eight Spitfires each from Nos. 126, 185, and 229 (Takali) Sqns are scrambled to intercept. JG 53's Bf 109s attack No. 185 Sqn Spitfires 25 miles north of Malta, shooting down one.

7. 1315–1330hrs: as the Ju 88s approach from the east, eight Spitfires from No. 229 Sqn intercept. C.202s and Bf 109s damage two Spitfires that later crash-land. The Ju 88s bomb around Luqa.

8. 1330–1345hrs: ten Spitfires from Nos. 126 and 185 Sqns pounce on the Ju 88s heading home, damaging one that later crash-lands at base. A C.202 is also shot down before combat is broken off.

9. 1550–1630hrs: seven Ju 88s, escorted by 30 C.202s and 42 Bf 109s, approach for an attack on Qrendi. Eight Spitfires each from Nos. 249, 229, and 1435 Sqns are scrambled. Twenty miles north of Gozo, the attackers meet the eight Spitfires of No. 249 Sqn. A Ju 88 and a C.202 are shot down.

10. 1630–1650hrs: the remaining Ju 88s bomb around Qrendi. As the attackers head for home, they are intercepted by the Spitfires of Nos. 229 and 1435 Sqns. A second Ju 88 and another C.202 are lost. Two Spitfires are damaged and crash upon landing.

LUFTWAFFE AND REGIA AERONAUTICA UNITS ⬤

1. II./LG 1, escorted by I./JG 77
2. III./KG 77, escorted by 153° Gruppo and I./JG 77
3. II./LG 1, escorted by 20° and 155° Gruppi and II./JG 53
4. Ju 88s, escorted by 20°, 153°, and 155° Gruppi, and II./JG 53 and I./JG 77

RAF UNITS ⬤

A. No. 185 Squadron
B. No. 249 Squadron
C. No. 1435 Squadron
D. No. 126 Squadrdon
E. No. 229 Squadron

The final blitz against Malta

13 October 1942

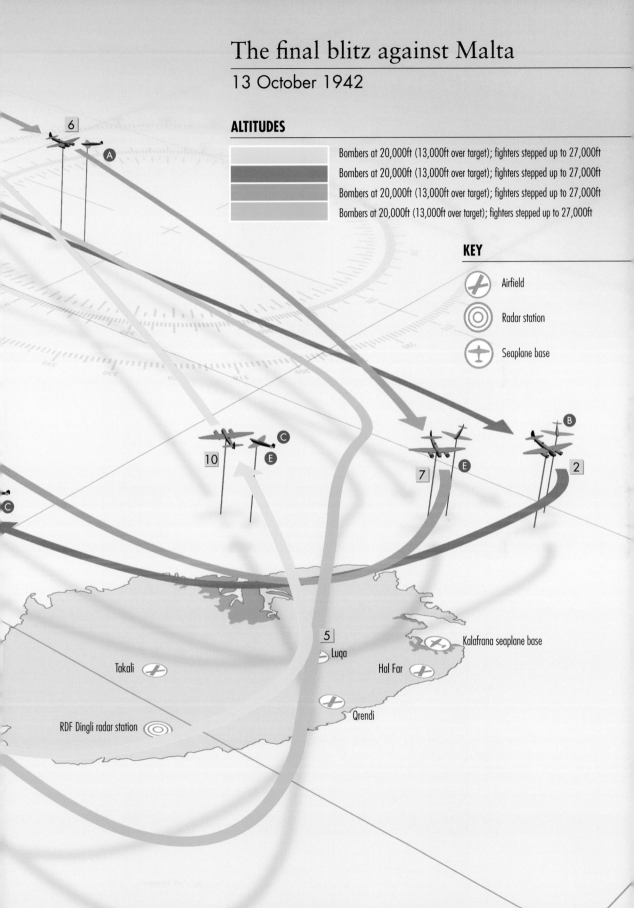

ALTITUDES

	Bombers at 20,000ft (13,000ft over target); fighters stepped up to 27,000ft
	Bombers at 20,000ft (13,000ft over target); fighters stepped up to 27,000ft
	Bombers at 20,000ft (13,000ft over target); fighters stepped up to 27,000ft
	Bombers at 20,000ft (13,000ft over target); fighters stepped up to 27,000ft

KEY

Airfield

Radar station

Seaplane base

Kalafrana seaplane base

Luqa

Hal Far

Takali

Qrendi

RDF Dingli radar station

ANALYSIS

Winston Churchill inspecting bomb damage in Valletta during a visit to Malta on 19 November 1943. The RAF's sacrifice in contesting the Axis' control of the skies over Malta was not minimal: from 1940 until the Allied invasion of Italy, 547 aircraft from Malta were destroyed in the air, around 160 on the ground, and 2,301 airmen lost their lives. In addition over 1,300 civilian perished in the campaign. (Lt D.C. Oulds/IWM via Getty Images)

The two fundamental reasons that best explain the Axis' failure to effectively neutralize and later occupy Malta over the two-year campaign are that firstly, the Regia Aeronautica alone proved to be incapable of conducting an effective aerial denial campaign against the island; and secondly, the Luftwaffe was not allowed by Hitler and the OKW to complete an effective aerial denial campaign. The greatest problem for the Regia Aeronautica was that it was thrown into a campaign, let alone a war, for which it was simply not prepared. It failed to realize that its early neutralization raids against Malta were simply not heavy or regular enough to impose aerial denial over the island. Initial lack of RAF activity and reinforcements was misinterpreted as operational success. When this error was realized in the autumn of 1940, it was too late to remedy as Regia Aeronautica resources became heavily committed in North Africa and Greece, two additional campaigns which had not been properly planned for. The Italian aviation industry's inability to effectively replace combat losses and its failure to mass-produce a new generation of medium bombers as capable as the Ju 88 meant that the Regia Aeronautica could never assemble as large and as effective an offensive force as that of Loerzer's II Fliegerkorps.

The offensive capability of the Regia Aeronautica was also marginalized by the limited capabilities and combat techniques of its increasingly obsolescent medium bomber force. This was demonstrated by the minimal and ineffective nocturnal bombardment campaigns waged by the Aeronautica della Sicilia against Malta in the second half of 1941 and the first half of 1942. The Regia Aeronautica entered World War II prepared only for a short and limited conflict; it lacked the aircraft, effective tactical development, and clearly defined mission objectives to effectively fight a long war in multiple theatres across the length of the Mediterranean basin. Mussolini, who overconfidently led the charge against the British in the Mediterranean in the summer of 1940, was eventually forced to submit to the strategic imperatives of his German ally; the quest for *Mare Nostrum* ultimately became a fight for survival.

The outcome of the Luftwaffe's campaigns against Malta was decided by Hitler's lack of a committed strategy for the Mediterranean theatre. In some ways the Axis air campaign against Malta resembled the Battle of Britain in microcosm – most certainly in that the course of the campaign was determined by Hitler's lack of commitment to achieving a tangible strategic goal and his preoccupation with other fronts and operations. The Luftwaffe had the aircraft and tactics necessary to obtain air superiority over the central Mediterranean and in the spring of 1941 and the spring of 1942 it proved it could neutralize Malta's aerial and naval offensive capabilities. However, in terms of overall strategic impact, the Luftwaffe's units in Sicily ended up performing the role of emergency firefighter, extinguishing the fires in the central Mediterranean that the Italians could not control. This was certainly how Hitler viewed the role of the Luftwaffe in the theatre and it skewed his overall assessment of Italian military capabilities. Ultimately it was Hitler's willingness to ignore the strategic importance of Malta to the Mediterranean theatre and his refusal to commit to an invasion that allowed the island and the forces based there to play an important role in the final defeat of the Axis powers in North Africa and the Mediterranean. Sadly for the brave pilots and air crews of the Regia Aeronautica and the Luftwaffe, and fortunately for those of the RAF defenders, the Axis aerial campaign against Malta became a textbook example of defeat being snatched from the jaws of victory. By May 1942 aerial denial was achieved, and then Hitler simply walked away.

CANT Z.1007 *bis* flying over British warships on fire in the central Mediterranean in the summer of 1942. Over the course of the summer Kesselring shifted Axis aerial efforts against British convoys to Malta, which in turn allowed the RAF to rebuild and eventually reassert air superiority over the island by the autumn. (Keystone/Getty Images)

APPENDICES

Italian airfields on Sicily and units deployed against Malta

Regia Aeronautica units (listed at their primary airfield of operation)

CASTELVETRANO		
2° Gruppo C.T. (150a, 152a, 358a Squadriglie)	Re.2001	Jun 1942–Jul 1942
4° Gruppo aut. A.S. (14a, 15a, Squadriglie)	SM.84	Aug 1942–Oct 1942
9° Gruppo C.T. (73a, 96a, 97a Squadriglie)	C.202	Apr 1942
16° Gruppo C.T. (167a, 168a, 169a Squadriglie)	C.200/C.202	Jul 1942
20° Gruppo C.T. (151a, 352a, 353a Squadriglie)	C.202	Nov 1942–Dec 1942
25° Gruppo B.T. (8a, 9a Squadriglie)	SM.84	Jul 1942–Sep 1942
33° Gruppo B.T. (59a, 60a Squadriglie)	Z.1007 bis	Sep 1942–Nov 1942
55° Gruppo B.T. (220a, 221a Squadriglie)	BR.20M	Apr 1942–May 1942
88° Gruppo B.T. (264a, 265a Squadriglie)	BR.20M	May 1942–Aug 1942
108° Gruppo B.T. (256a, 257a Squadriglie)	SM.79	Jun 1940–Nov 1940
109° Gruppo B.T. (258a, 259a Squadriglie)	SM.79	Jun 1940
116° Gruppo B.T. (276a, 277a Squadriglie)	BR.20M	Jun 1942–Jul 1942
132° Gruppo aut. A.S. (278a Squadriglia)	SM.79	Apr 1942–Jun 1942

CATANIA		
279a Squadriglia aut. A.S.	SM.79	Dec 1940–Apr 1941
6° Gruppo aut. C.T. (79a, 81a, 88a Squadriglie)	C.200	Jun 1940–Jun 1941
31° Gruppo B.T. (65a, 66a Squadriglie)	BR.20M	Jun 1941–Oct 1941
52° Gruppo B.T. (214a. 215a Squadriglie)	SM.79	Jun 1940–Dec 1940
53° Gruppo B.T. (216a, 217a Squadriglie)	SM.79	Jun 1940–Dec 1940
105° Gruppo B.T. (254a, 255a Squadriglie)	SM.79	Aug 1940–Sep 1940
116° Gruppo B.T. (276a, 277a Squadriglie)	BR.20M	Oct 1940–Nov 1941
130° Gruppo aut. A.S. (280a, 283a Squadriglie)	SM.79	Mar 1942–Apr 1942

CHINISIA		
2° Gruppo C.T. (150a, 152a, 358a Squadriglie)	Re.2001	Aug 1942–Jan 1943
3° Gruppo C.T. (153a, 154a, 155a Squadriglie)	C.200	Nov 1942–May 1943
10° Gruppo C.T. (84a, 90a, 91a Squadriglie)	C.200	Nov 1941–Dec 1941
29° Gruppo B.T. (62a, 63a Squadriglie)	Z.1007 bis	Sep 1941–Jan 1942; Jun 1942–May 1943
32° Gruppo B.T. (57a, 58a Squadriglie)	SM.79	Apr 1941–Jun 1942
33° Gruppo B.T. (59a, 60a Squadriglie)	Z.1007 bis	Aug 1941–Jan 1942; May 1942–Sep 1942
151° Gruppo C.T. (366a, 377a, 378a)	G.50	Nov 1942–May 1943
153° Gruppo C.T. (372a, 373a, 374a Squadriglie)	C.202	Oct 1942–Nov 1942

OPPOSITE The Supermarine Spitfire Mark V of Air Vice Marshal Park climbs away from Safi on 15 May 1943 to mark the airfield's official opening. Although construction had begun in 1941 and the strip became operational in 1942, it was not until the Axis campaign had ended that this ceremonial opening took place. (Photo by Flying Officer G. Woodbine/IWM via Getty Images)

COMISO		
7° Gruppo C.T. (76a, 86a, 98a Squadriglie)	C.200	May 1941–Jun 1941
9° Gruppo C.T. (73a, 96a, 97a Squadriglie)	CR.42/C.202	Jul 1940; Sep 1941–Nov 1941
10° Gruppo C.T. (84a, 90a, 91a Squadriglie)	C.200	Sep 1941–Nov 1941
23° Gruppo C.T. (70a, 74a, 75a Squadriglie)	CR.42	Jul 1940–Dec 1940; Mar 1941–Apr 1941
33° Gruppo B.T. (59a, 60a Squadriglie)	SM.79	Jun 1940–Jul 1940
34° Gruppo B.T. (67a, 68a Squadriglie)	SM.79	Jun 1940
96° Gruppo B.a.T. (236a, 237a Squadriglie)	Ju 87	Aug 1940–Oct 1940; Jan 1941
97° Gruppo B.a.T. (238a, 239a Squadriglie)	Ju 87	Nov 1940–Dec 1940
156° Gruppo C.T. (379a, 380a Squadriglie)	CR.42	Jan 1941–Apr 1941 (absorbed into 23° Gruppo C.T.)

GELA		
16° Gruppo C.T. (167a, 168a, 169a Squadriglie)	C.200	Jun 1941
20° Gruppo C.T. (151a, 352a, 353a Squadriglie)	C.202	Jun 1942–Nov 1942
22° Gruppo C.T. (359a, 362a, 369a Squadriglie)	Re.2001	Sep 1942–Nov 1942
59° Gruppo B.T. (232a, 233a Squadriglie)	SM.79	Jun 1940–Oct 1940
60° Gruppo B.T. (234a, 235a Squadriglie)	SM.79	Jun 1940–Oct 1940
102° Gruppo B.a.T. (209a, 239a Squadriglie)	Ju 87R	May 1942–Oct 1942
155° Gruppo C.T. (351a, 360a, 378a Squadriglie)	C.202	May 1942–Nov 1942; Dec 1942
171° Gruppo aut. C.N. (301a, 302a Squadriglie)	CR.42	Oct 1941

GERBINI		
281a Squadriglia A.S. (132° Gruppo aut. A.S.)	SM.79	May 1942
282a Squadriglia aut. A.S.	SM.79	Jul 1941–Nov 1941
16° Gruppo C.T. (167a, 168a, 169a Squadriglie)	C.200	Jul 1941–Jun 1942
55° Gruppo B.T. (220a, 221a Squadriglie)	BR.20M	May 1941–Dec 1941
88° Gruppo B.T. (264a, 265a Squadriglie)	BR.20M	Aug 1942–Nov 1942
99° Gruppo B.T. (242a, 243a Squadriglie)	BR.20M	May 1941–Jul 1942
101° Gruppo B.a.T. (208a, 238a Squadriglie)	Ju 87	Jul 1942

PALERMO		
173a Squadriglia aut. R.S.T.	CR.25	Jul 1941–Jan 1942 (merged into 10° Stormo)
17° Gruppo C.T. (71a, 72a, 80a Squadriglie)	CR.32	Jun 1940–Sep 1940
30° Gruppo B.T. (55a, 56a Squadriglie)	SM.79/SM.84	Jun 1942–Aug 1942; Nov 1942–May 1943
32° Gruppo B.T. (57a, 58a Squadriglie)	Ca.314	Jun 1942–May 1943

PANTELLERIA		
278a Squadriglia A.S.	SM.79	Feb 1941–Mar 1942
2° Gruppo C.T. (150a, 152a, 358a Squadriglie)	Re.2001	Jun 1942–Jul 1942
6° Gruppo C.T. (79a, 81a, 88a Squadriglie)	C.202	Nov 1942–Dec 1942
7° Gruppo C.T. (76a, 86a, 98a Squadriglie)	C.200	Jun 1941–Jul 1942
101° Gruppo B.a.T. (208a, 238a Squadriglie)	Ju 87	Jul 1942
130° Gruppo aut. A.S. (280a, 283a Squadriglie)	SM.79	Apr 1942–May 1942

SAN PIETRO A CALTAGIRONE		
2° Gruppo C.T. (150a, 152a, 358a Squadriglie)	Re.2001	May 1942–Jun 1942
153° Gruppo C.T. (372a, 373a, 374a Squadriglie)	C.202	Sep 1942–Oct 1942

SCIACCA		
10° Gruppo C.T. (84a, 90a, 91a Squadriglie)	C.202	Apr 1942
30° Gruppo B.T. (55a, 56a Squadriglie)	SM.79	Apr 1941–Jun 1942; Aug 1942–Oct 1942
87° Gruppo B.T. (192a, 193a Squadriglie)	SM.79	Jun 1940–Aug 1941
90° Gruppo B.T. (194a, 195a Squadriglie)	SM.79	Jun 1940–Sep 1941

TRAPANI		
377a Squadriglia aut. C.T.	Re.2000	Jul 1941
10° Gruppo C.T. (84a, 90a, 91a Squadriglie)	C.200	Jun 1941–Sep 1941
17° Gruppo C.T. (71a, 72a, 80a Squadriglie)	C.200	Sep 1940–Jun 1941
33° Gruppo B.T. (59a, 60a Squadriglie)	Z.1007 bis	Jun 1941–Aug 1941
101° Gruppo B.a.T. (208a, 238a Squadriglie)	Ju 87	May 1941–Dec 1941
106° Gruppo B.T. (260a, 261a Squadriglie)	Z.1007	Aug 1940
157° Gruppo C.T. (384a, 385a, 386a Squadriglie)	CR.42	Jun 1940–Dec 1940

Luftwaffe units (listed at their primary airfield of operation)

CATANIA		
1.(F)/Aufklärungsgruppe 121	Ju 88D	Dec 1940–Jun 1941
1.(F)/Aufklärungsgruppe 122	Ju 88D	Apr 1942–Dec 1942
2.(F)/Aufklärungsgruppe 123	Ju 88D	Feb 1941–Jun 1941
Stab/Kampfgeschwader 54	Ju 88A	Dec 1941–May 1943
I./ Kampfgeschwader 54	Ju 88A	Sep 1942–Dec 1942
II./ Kampfgeschwader 54	Ju 88A	Oct 1942–May 1943
III./ Kampfgeschwader 54	Ju 88A	Sep 1942–Feb 1943
I./ Kampfgeschwader 77	Ju 88A	Sep 1942–Mar 1943
II./ Kampfgeschwader 100	He 111H	Oct 1942–Nov 1942
Kampfgruppe 606	Ju 88A	Dec 1941–Sep 1942
II./Lehrgeschwader 1	Ju 88A	Jan 1941–May 1941; Mar 1942–Jun 1942; Oct 1942–Nov 1942
III./Lehrgeschwader 1	Ju 88A	Jan 1941–May 1941
I./ Nachtjagdgeschwader 2	Ju 88C	Nov 1941–Sep 1942

COMISO		
I./ Jagdgeschwader 27	Bf 109E	Mar 1941
Stab/Jagdgeschwader 53	Bf 109F/G	Dec 1941–Nov 1942
II./Jagdgeschwader 53	Bf 109F/G	Dec 1941–Nov 1942
III./Jagdgeschwader 53	Bf 109F	Dec 1941–May 1942
I./ Jagdgeschwader 77	Bf 109F/G	Jul 1942–Oct 1942
2./Kampfgeschwader 4	He 111H	Jan 1941–May 1941
II./Kampfgeschwader 26	He 111H	Jan 1941–May 1941
I./ Kampfgeschwader 54	Ju 88A	May 1942–Jul 1942
Stab/Kampfgeschwader 77	Ju 88A	Dec 1941–Apr 1942; Jul 1942–Dec 1942
II./ Kampfgeschwader 77	Ju 88A	Dec 1941–May 1942; Jul 1942
I./ Schlachtgeschwader 2	Bf 109F	Sep 1942–Oct 1942

GELA		
7./Jagdgeschwader 26	Bf 109E	Feb 1941–May 1941
III./Jagdgeschwader 27	Bf 109E	May 1941
I./Jagdgeschwader 53	Bf 109F	Dec 1941–Apr 1942
10.(Jabo)/Jagdgeschwader 53	Bf 109F-4B	May 1942–Jun 1942
1./ Nachtjagdgeschwader 3	Bf 110C	Feb 1941–May 1941

GERBINI		
1.(F)/Aufklärungsgruppe 122	Ju 88D	Feb 1942–Apr 1942
III./Kampfgeschwader 30	Ju 88A	Feb 1941–Jun 1941
I./ Kampfgeschwader 54	Ju 88A	Dec 1941–May 1942; Jul 1942–Sep 1942
II./ Kampfgeschwader 77	Ju 88A	Oct 1942–Dec 1942
III./ Kampfgeschwader 77	Ju 88A	Oct 1942–Dec 1942

PALERMO		
III./Zerstörergeschwader 26	Bf 110C	Dec 1940–Jan 1941

SAN PIETRO A CALTAGIRONE		
II./Jagdgeschwader 3	Bf 109F	Feb 1942–Apr 1942
Jabostaffel/Jagdgeschwader 3	Bf 109F-2/B	Mar 1942–Apr 1942
10.(Jabo)/Jagdgeschwader 53	Bf 109F-4B	Mar 1942–May 1942
III./ Sturzkampfgeschwader 3	Ju 87R	Mar 1942–May 1942

SCIACCA		
II./Jagdgeschwader 3	Bf 109F	Jan 1942–Feb 1942

TRAPANI		
I./ Sturzkampfgeschwader 1	Ju 87R	Dec 1940–Feb 1941
III./ Sturzkampfgeschwader 1	Ju 87R	Feb 1941–Mar 1941
II./ Sturzkampfgeschwader 2	Ju 87R	Dec 1940–Feb 1941
III./Zerstörergeschwader 26	Bf 110C	Jan 1941–May 1942

*note – excluded are Regia Aeronautica and Luftwaffe air-sea rescue and transport units.

BIBLIOGRAPHY

Apostolo, Giorgio, *FIAT CR 42*, Torino: La Bancarella Aeronautica, 1995

Austin, Douglas, *Malta and British Strategic Policy 1925–43*, London: Frank Cass, 2004

Badoglio, Pietro, *Italy in the Second World War: Memories and Documents*, London: Oxford University Press, 1948

Boog, Horst, Werner Rahn, Reinhard Stumpf, and Bernd Wegner (eds), *Germany and the Second World War. Volume VI: The Global War: Widening of the Conflict into a World War and the Shift of the Initiative 1941–1943*, Oxford: Clarendon Press, 2001

Botti, Ferruccio, 'La Guerra Aerea: Strategia d'impiego: concezioni contrastanti.' *L'Italia in Guerra. Il 1° anno – 1940*, edited by R. H. Rainero and A. Biagini, Roma: Commissione Italiana di Storia Militare, 1991: pp. 215–243

Budden, Michael J., 'Defending the Indefensible? The Air Defense of Malta, 1936–1940', *War in History*, Vol. 6, No. 4 (1999): pp. 447–467

Cattaneo, Gianni, *AerMacchi C.200*, Torino: La Bancarella Aeronautica, 1997

Curami, Andrea, 'Commesse belliche e approvvigionamenti di materie prime', *L'Italia in Guerra. Il 1° anno – 1940*, edited by R. H. Rainero and A. Biagini, Roma: Commissione Italiana di Storia Militare, 1991: pp. 55-68.

Curami, Andrea, 'Piani e progetti dell'aeronautica italiana 1939–1943: Stato maggiore e industrie.' *Italia contemporanea* 187 (June 1992): pp. 243–61.

Departments of the Army and the Air Force, *German Explosive Ordnance*, Washington D.C.: United States Government Printing Office, 1953

Departments of the Army and the Air Force, *Italian and French Explosive Ordnance*, Washington D.C.: United States Government Printing Office, 1953

Dierich, Wolfgang, ed., *Die Verbände der Luftwaffe 1935–1945: Gliederungen und Kurzchroniken – Eine Dokumentation*, Stuttgart: Motorbuch Verlag, 1976

Dunning, Chris, *Regia Aeronautica: The Italian Air Force 1923–1945 – An Operational History*, Hersham: Ian Allan Publishing, 2009

Felmy, Helmuth, *The German Air Force in the Mediterranean Theater of War.* United States Air Force Historical Study 161, Washington D.C.: United States Air Force, 1955

Ferrari, Paolo, *L'aeronautica Italiana: Una Storia Del Novecento*, Milano: F. Angeli, 2004

Forczyk, Robert, *We March Against England: Operation Sea Lion, 1940–41*, Oxford: Osprey Publishing, 2016

Gabriele, Mariano, 'L'Offensiva su malta (1941),' in *L'Italia in Guerra: Il secondo anno – 1941*, edited by R. H. Rainero and A. Biagini, Roma Commissione Italiana di Storia Militare, 1992: pp. 435–450.

Gabriele, Mariano, 'L'Operazione 'C3' (1942),' in *L'Italia in Guerra: Il 3° anno – 1942*, edited by R. H. Rainero and A. Biagini, Roma: Commissione Italiana di Storia Militare, 1993: pp. 409–434

Garello, Giancarlo, *C.R.D.A. Cant Z.1007*, La Bancarella Aeronautica, 2002

Gori, Cesare, *SIAI S.79: 1a parte.* Torino: La Bancarella Aeronautica, 1998

Greene, Jack and Alessandro Massignani, *The Naval War in the Mediterranean 1940–1943*, London: Chatham Publishing, 1998

Gundelach, Karl, *Die deutsche Luftwaffe im Mittelmeer 1940–45: Band I*, Frankfurt am Main: Peter D. Lang, 1981

Higham, Robin, and Stephen J. Harris., *Why Air Forces Fail: The Anatomy of Defeat*, Lexington: The University Press of Kentucky, 2006

Hudson, S.A.M., *UXB Malta: Royal Engineers Bomb Disposal 1940–44*, Stroud: Spellmount, 2010

Kens, Karlheinz and Heinz J. Nowarra, *Die Deutschen Flugzeuge 1933–1945: Deutschlands Luftfahrt-Entwicklungen Bis Zum Ende Des Zweiten Weltkrieges*, München: Lehmanns Verlag, 1977

Knox, MacGregor, *Hitler's Italian Allies: Royal Armed Force, Fascist Regime, and the War of 1940–43*, Cambridge: Cambridge University Press, 2000

Kreis, John F., *Air Warfare and Air Base Air Defense, 1914–1973*, Washington D.C.: Office of Air Force History, United States Air Force, 1988

Larrazábal, J.S., *Das Flugzeug im Spanischen Bürgerkrieg*, Stuttgart: Motorbuch Verlag, 1973

Maiolo, Joseph, *Cry Havoc: How the Arms Race Drove the World to War, 1931–1941*, New York: Basic Books, 2010

Malizia, Nicola, *Inferno su Malta: La piú lunga battaglia aeronavale della seconda Guerra mondiale*, Milano: U. Mursia editore, 1976

Malizia, Nicola, *La Regia Aeronautica nella 2a guerra mondiale: Dai diari di guerra: 1940–1942*, Rome: IBN Editore, 2013

Mallett, Robert, *The Italian Navy and Fascist Expansionism, 1935–40*, London: Frank Cass, 1998

Millett, Allan R. and Williamson Murray, (eds), *Military Effectiveness. Volume II: The Interwar Period*, Boston: Allan & Unwin, 1988

Minniti, Fortunato, 'Il problema degli armament nella preparazione militaire italiana dal 1935 al 1943', *Storia contemporanea*, Vol. 9, No. 11 (1978): pp. 5–61

Morewood, Steven, 'The Chiefs of Staff, the 'men on the spot' and the Italo-Abyssinian Emergency, 1935–36,' in *Decisions and Diplomacy: Essays in Twentieth-Century International History*, edited by Dick Richardson and Glyn Stone, London: Routledge, 2005: pp. 85–110

Philpott, Ian, *The Royal Air Force: An Encyclopedia of the Inter-War Years. Volume II: Rearmament 1930–1939*. Barnsley: Pen & Sword, 2008

Pricolo, Francesco, *La Regia Aeronautica nella seconda guerra mondiale: novembre 1939–novembre 1941*, Milano: Longanesi & C., 1971

Rocca, Gianni. *I disperati. La tragedia dell'aeronautica italiana nella seconda guerra mondiale*. Milano: Arnoldo Mondadori Editore S.p.A., 1991.

Rollo, Denis, *The Guns and Gunners of Malta*, Marsa: Mondial Publishers, 1999

Santoro, Giuseppe, *L'Aeronautica italiana nella seconda guerra mondiale*, Roma: Apollon, 1957

Schreiber, Gerhard, Bernd Stegemann, and Detlef Vogel (eds), *Germany and the Second World War, Volume III: The Mediterranean, South-east Europe, and North Africa 1939–1941*, Oxford: Clarendon Press, 1995

Sganga, Rodolfo, Paulo G. Tripodi, and Wray R. Johnson, 'Douhet's Antagonist: Amedeo Mecozzi's Alternative Vision of Air Power,' *Air Power History*, Vol. 58, No. 2 (2011): pp. 4–15

Shores, Christopher and Brian Cull with Nicola Malizia, *Malta: The Hurricane Years 1940–41*, London: Grub Street, 1987

Shores, Christopher and Brian Cull with Nicola Malizia, *Malta: The Spitfire Year 1942*, London: Grub Street, 1991

Smith, J.R. and Antony L. Kay, *German Aircraft of the Second World War*, London: Putnam Aeronautical Books, 1972

Spooner, Tony, *Supreme Gallantry: Malta's Role in the Allied Victory 1939–1945*, London: John Murray, 1996

Waldis, Paolo and Ferdinando Pedriali, *FIAT BR.20. 1a parte*, Torino: La Bancarella Aeronautica, 2006

INDEX